Mindset
Open Your Mind to New Possibilities

Ellis Hodge

RIVER BIRCH PRESS
Mobile, Alabama

ISBN 978-1-951561-42-0 (print)
ISBN 978-1-951561-43-7 (e-book)
For Worldwide Distribution
Printed in the U.S.A.

River Birch Press
P.O. Box 828
Daphne, AL 36526

Table of Contents

Dedication   *iv*

Foreword   *v*

Introduction   *vi*

1   New Mindset—Ephesians 4:17-22   *1*

2   The Blessing of a Humble Mindset—James 4:6-8   *26*

3   Putting on a New Mindset—Romans 12:2   *48*

4   Having a Jesus Mindset—Philippians 2:1-2   *68*

5   Having a Jesus Mindset, Part II—Philippians 2:3-4   *87*

6   Having a Jesus Mindset, Part III—Philippians 2:7-9   *104*

7   A Word-Working Mindset—Romans 12:2   *119*

8   A Purified Mindset—Ephesians 4:17-19   *137*

To my lovely wife
who has always said to me,
"You can do anything you put your mind to
when you really want to do it."
I also want to acknowledge
my mother, Elizabeth Hodge,
and my grandmother, Hattie Franklin,
who always told me,
"If anything is worth doing,
it is worth doing right."

Foreword

I would like to recommend the new book by my very good friend, Dr. Ellis Hodge, entitled *Mindset*. I have always known that Dr. Hodge is a great leader of men, and the whole family, with his congregation at Word of Life Fellowship in St. Petersburg, Florida. But in the process of time, I have watched as he has developed into an amazing community leader, greatly expanding his sphere of influence. It is from this unique perspective that he gives readers a truly balanced approach to developing a lifestyle that will, in turn, have others see them as a true leader in both the church and the community environment.

The secret to Dr. Hodge's wisdom is developing and maintaining a fixed mindset based on seeing everything the way God does. I kept sensing as I read his book that God will greatly use Dr. Hodge's instructions to help many men and women go through the process that the Bible calls the "transformation of life, by the renewing of your mind." Dr. Hodge uses very common sense applications of God's Word to various familiar experiences in life that can save people from crashing and burning, to use an old expression, and respond to life's challenges the way that God would have them respond. Afterward, they will gain completely different and successful results.

If you have ever wondered how great leaders maintain their ability to remain consistent in the midst of great external opposition and always come out smelling like a rose, read and meditate on Dr. Ellis Hodge's new book, *Mindset*.
—*Dr. Douglas J. Wingate, President and Founder of Life Christian University, a global ministry education university*

Introduction

The purpose in writing this book is to encourage believers and others to come to an understanding that following and living our lives according to and by the word of God requires a new mindset. To know also that the word of God compels all of us, believers and non-believers to...

1. Obtain and maintain a very clear understanding of God's Word from God's Word.

2. By obtaining the understanding of God's Word, you make a decision to make Jesus your Lord and Savior, thereby making the Word of God the standard by which you will live your life.

1

NEW MINDSET
Ephesians 4:17-22

We esteem You, God, because You are truly worthy. We do it not only because of what You have done or where You are but because of *who* You are. We choose to magnify You today, all the while thanking You for who You are to us. We are so grateful and appreciative of all You have given us. We thank You for all of your promises, Your faithfulness, and Your Word. We thank You for the simple fact that we have the blood of Jesus, and that it's a cleansing mechanism that continually purges us from sin and its works.

We thank You again for Your Word, as You guide us while we navigate our way through this life. We thank You that You are always keeping us on the right path and teaching us how to walk the trail You have chosen for us. Thank You for the Holy Spirit, who is our true Guide, who speaks to us and gives us clear direction when we don't know what we should do, how we should do it, or where we should go.

God, You have done it all. It is finished. We thank You so much for what You have made available to us. We thank You so much for what You have given to us as Your children. God, we thank You that You didn't base it on our worth. Everything you've shared with us has its roots in love, and we thank You that Your love moved You to do for us what we truly needed, rather than just allowing us to get what we merely wanted. We bless You, and we praise You endlessly.

Our deepest desire at this moment is to learn more about You, God. We desire to be instructed and taught. Your guidance is not for us to sit on but to use in our lives. We, as your children, decide right now to put everything You pour into us to good use. We will make every effort to ensure that this gift of Your teaching, this gift of knowledge, this gift of understanding can be manifested in our lives so that the world will see us and glorify You. Instruct us by Your Spirit, as we say this prayer in Jesus' name.

In this book, we will examine and discuss a *new mindset,* and what it would mean for our lives if we would adopt the new mindset. If anyone has real knowledge when it comes to this mindset idea, Paul the apostle is the right person to inform us.

In Ephesians, Paul writes to the church in that city. These are actual believers that Paul was writing to, not just random people on the street. If you will keep this thought in the back of your mind while you read this book, I believe it will help us understand precisely where Paul is coming from, and how everything he says still applies to us today.

I believe this world is filled to the brim with believers who don't quite understand how wealthy they are as children of God. Believers are always striving for something else, looking out at the world and trying to capture the next thing they believe is needed to be truly happy. There are tons of people like this today, but from what Paul wrote, we can tell that this same mistake was made all the way back to the days of Jesus. The grave misconception is that we don't utilize what has been made available to us in Jesus because we can't see what is in front of us.

God has availed Himself of everything He is, of everything He has and made an offering of it to us. *Everything.* We have at our disposal the information and the power to live a completely different life than we currently live. We also can have the attitude and mindset to radically change the dynamics of our lives, but only if we choose to do so.

When we come into this world, we don't know what we possess. How are we supposed to know except we are taught? And to be honest with you, the way God interacts with us now is pretty unbelievable. Men have lived on this earth for a while, making mistakes every day. But even still, when we come to God, He says, "Okay, if you work with Me, you and I can turn your whole situation around." Together with God, we can point our lives in a totally different direction. But as you know, it takes a new kind of mindset to wrap our heads around that idea and put it to work.

This reminds me of a particular childhood memory that has stuck with me through the years. When I was a kid, there used to be a TV show called *The Million Dollar Man.*

This guy would go around delivering checks for a million bucks! When he got to the doorstep, he'd say, "My name is so-and-so, and I'm here because my boss wants to give you a million dollars!" Sometimes, he would have to run people down and force them to accept the money. Why? They just couldn't believe it. They actually thought the guy was out of his mind! And the whole time I was watching this, I was thinking, "Just come to my door! You won't have to twist my arm, I promise."

This scenario parallels the way we look at God's gifts to us. We've been trained to think a certain way for our entire lives, and our mindsets are set in stone. When God comes along and says, "Here's a gift that has the capacity to change your life and transform it into something better than you could ever imagine," we react in an incredulous and uncooperative manner. We say things like, "Personally, I've been doing this throughout my entire life." People hate change because it forces them to abandon what is comfortable and adopt a brand new mindset. Because of having to change, we choose to remain stuck and stay in what is comfortable and what we are familiar with.

We don't like change. In fact, we can't stand it, so we fight it tooth and nail. We get so comfortable in our emotions and our way of thinking that we don't want to budge for anything or anyone. But when you serve a God like the God we serve, you're going to be challenged and stretched. He will never allow you to stay in one spot for too long because you'll get complacent and lose sight of what's really important. That is why the children of Israel had difficulty following and obeying God. Slavery overtook their mindset, and they had trouble releasing that idea when they finally became free. Think of it this way: You may not have the physical symbols of slavery, like shackles and chains, but you may still be imprisoned in your mind or thinking.

Have you ever heard the term institutionalized? It applies to all sorts of folks, like people who just can't seem to stay out of jail. Right after they get released, they wind up back in their same old cell. They have been in prison or jail for so long that the only place where they can actually function is when they are locked up. That's the life they've come to know. They are fed at certain times, they shower at certain times, and everything is streamlined and consistent. When they are released into the real world, they don't know how to make any sense of the chaos and unpredictable nature of fending for themselves, so they just go right back to jail. At least when they're locked up, they know what to expect.

You might say that's downright crazy, but why don't you try being locked up for 20 or 30 years? Stuck in a cell, with no way out, you'd develop a different kind of mindset. The believers that Paul was writing to in Ephesus mirror the church today. God has given us literally everything. Some of us are basking in His provision right this very moment, but we don't notice it. If we would get our mindset to align with the Holy Spirit, we could do a hundred times more than what Christ has already done in our lives.

Some of the believers in Ephesus had been around when Jesus was on the earth, and a few had actually witnessed some of the mercies He had shown us. This is like some of us in a way. We know God has power. We have seen Him at work, and we've been the fortunate recipients of some truly awesome miracles and the manifestation of God's power in our lives. But there is something about this thing between our ears that keeps us from fully embracing and accepting God's power. For example: we know God can heal our bodies, but time and time again, our mindset keeps us from receiving the healing. We have all of God's promises available to us, but our mindset is stuck in the old way of thinking. We're living in this healing, walking and talking and breathing in this healing, and everything is changing, but our mindset is still stuck in the old way of thinking. We can't move into the mindset where we fully believe. We keep operating in our old mindset. It is like in our thinking we live on the back street when we should be living on Main Street.

The reason we aren't grasping His miracles has nothing to do with God placing limitations on us. He's not withholding these gifts—He's telling us that they're all ours. We are still so insecure about all sorts of things and entirely too worried about what people say about us and how they feel about us. No matter what you do or how you act, you'll never get to a point where everyone approves. But we are so hung up on the opinions of others.

Can't we see how insane we are? "I don't really want people to know I have all of these blessings. I don't want people to feel like I think I'm better than they are." We embrace this poverty mindset; we'd rather starve and receive praise from the people around us than enjoy the provision that God has promised to us. Where's the sense in that? Why should I stay broke for the sake of other people's opinions of me? I'm not saying generosity isn't still a cornerstone. I am driving home a point: God is handing us beautiful gifts, and sometimes a false modesty or humility forces us to deny His kindness and refuse His gifts. We simply have to move past that.

Let's hop over to Romans 12. We will use this scripture as a springboard before moving back into Ephesians. Paul writes to the Roman church, "I beseech you, therefore, brethren, by the mercies of God..." We can all attest to that, right? We can understand that because God has been merciful towards each of us on an individual level. Some of us should have died two or three times by now, but we're still alive and kicking. God's mercy and His grace are undeniable.

The Bible says, "I beseech you, therefore, brethren, by the mercies of God, that ye present your bodies a living sacrifice, holy, acceptable unto God, which is your reasonable service" (Romans 12:1). Think about that phrase for a second: "a living sacrifice." We can't really relate to a dead sacrifice, because a dead sacrifice isn't bothered by anything or anyone around it. Paul basically says, "I want you to take it one step further. Make yourself a living sacrifice. I want you to be alive in the midst of sin and death but immune to them. The time of the dead sacrifice is over."

Now, it's a good thing to die for the Lord, but wouldn't it be a powerful statement if I served as a living sacrifice? I'm alive, and all the situations I face, all the people I encounter, don't sway me to turn my back on the way a child of God should behave. Paul says that you should present your body as a living sacrifice as holy and set aside. He gives us an example of what this living sacrifice looks like.

A person who is living their life as a living sacrifice to God understands that they are set aside and set apart.

This illustration might help: Do you have a favorite pair of shoes? Do you keep them in the box? Do you polish them and take good care of them? Most people only break out shoes like that when they're wearing an outfit that complements them. They don't see the light of day until that one particular outfit is summoned from the depths of their closet. You might have a few outfits that look similar. You might even have one or two that have the same color scheme, but they don't deserve those shoes. You don't crack that box open until you put that one outfit on. Nobody has to tell you how great you look in that moment. You just stare in the mirror and shout, "Man, I look so good! I can't stand myself!"

You set your absolute favorite pair of shoes aside for the special outfit, and you wait for an invitation to some fancy event so you can put them on. When you wear them, you already know the compliments are coming. "Where on earth did you get those beauties?" But you don't let anyone in on your secret.

So, when Paul talks about being holy and set apart for God's special purpose, you should understand that you are set aside and that being holy is being acceptable and pleasing in the eyes of God. I care about myself because I am set aside and holy. Holiness isn't necessarily piousness—its use here actually means acceptable or usable. What God sets aside is holy; it's sanctified; it has been purchased for a specific time and purpose. So, if this mechanism called the church is set aside, that means God has a special plan for the church, and we get to be a part of that plan.

Let's look at the next verse, Romans 12:2.

Be not conformed to this world: but be ye transformed by the renewing of your mind, that ye may prove what is that good, and acceptable, and perfect, will of God.

Now, there's a con-form, and there's a trans-form. A con-form is when I allow myself to be shaped and changed by my surroundings so that I fit into a specific mold. Sometimes we don't like where we're set apart because of all the temptation, but we have to stay focused.

If I truly understand in my mind and in my heart that I'm set apart, it doesn't matter what's going on around me. You don't want to participate? You don't have to. That does not mean you stop loving, though. That's a major misconception in our world today. People think that you don't like them if you're not hanging out with them. These days, we live in a world where everybody wants to be liked. You dare not tell anyone you don't want to hang out with them. They will immediately defend with something like, "What do you mean, you don't live like that? You think you're better than me?" It may be scary to face, and the friction may be uncomfortable, but that's the kind of thing you are going to have to deal with in this world as a child of God.

So, we shouldn't be con-formed, but rather be trans-formed. When Paul talks about the renewing of your mind, we come into contact with this concept of a healthier mindset.

My wife is very visual; she is able to see old dilapidated homes and visualize what they could look like. She said she learned it from her grandfather. When I think of the renewing of a mind, it helps to compare it to a contractor that is remodeling a home. He doesn't just concern himself with the outward appearance only; the contractor is also concerned with what the inside looks like also.

Instead, he guts the internal structure. Sure, the homeowner has an idea of what they want the room to look like. Of course, the first thing they say is that they want to repaint it. Styles change over time. Right now, we are in an era of loud colors. Back in the day, everything was just plain white—white ceiling, white walls—all-white everything. Why? Because it gave the illusion that the room was larger.

But now, through technological advancements and changes in design, we have found a way to paint a room multiple colors and still get the same effect. We have five-inch baseboards now, and it changes the whole feel of the room. You can make the ceiling one color, and the wall a different color, and it gives that same illusion.

It's remarkable to see something like that come together. The ceiling would be one color, and the walls would be another, but they would all work together to create this beautiful room. But, of course, you can't remodel a room without updating the electrical fixtures. You don't want ivory-colored fixtures, though. The whiter ones are better because they provide more contrast and make the walls pop. If you have a light blue wall, and you put some really white fixtures in there, the room begins to sing, "I'm looking good!"

Now, I'm not saying that God wants to change how you look—He probably wants you to keep your look! If you think your head is too big, He wants you to keep that big head. Right? But He needs to gut the inside in order to make you new. He has to knock down one way of thinking and tear out all of the internal stuff that came with it. He wants to remodel the room and make it exactly the way He wants it, so He can use us. That's a lot easier said than done. It's easier to remodel a room than it is to remodel our mind.

We love to say, "I just can't change." See, when you're in the construction business, and you set your sights on completing something by drawing up all the plans, you can't go back and change them every few minutes. You have to go with it. A lot of you say, "I just can't change like that. I'm not built like that." You're putting resistance into remodeling—something that is already hard enough as it is without you fighting it. Your mouth is causing resistance. It's not that you can't change, it's just that you *don't want to*. You have reached a level of comfort that you enjoy, and you don't want to give that up for anything under the sun.

The slaves liked Egypt. They thought, "We eat three square meals a day here. We have a place to sleep. Nothing's wrong with Egypt!" There's nothing wrong with a little welfare. But there is something wrong with it if it's doing something to your thinking. Back in the day, when welfare was just getting started, my mother was a recipient because she had a house full of children. It was an institution in America that was designed to tear families apart.

They said, "We can take care of women and children, but we are not going to take care of the husband." A lot of men left their families, thinking they were doing them a favor, but the welfare system moved in and became the father. Then, the real father went off and started another family, and the same thing happened there. Even today, the idea is, "We can help her, but we can't help her with a husband there." So now, women want to have a guy live with them because they want a man in the house, but they don't want to lose that check.

It becomes a trap. If she marries the man, the money stops rolling in. Women are sneaking men into their homes. It creates a different kind of mindset surrounding relationships and marriage. We have to connive and scheme in order to use the welfare system.

Even men get on welfare. Everyone wants in on the action, but no one realized it was slowly changing their mindset. Welfare changes your thinking. Men left their families thinking, "Well, if my wife can get a check for herself and the kids, and they're going to pay the rent, that means I don't have to pay it." He doesn't realize that being present with his family and broke was better than her getting a check without a father or husband in the picture. Fathers didn't know that. Fathers didn't see that. Fathers thought they were helping their family. But in the end, they were handing them over to a system that was going to wreak havoc on families in the future. No one thought that, years later, we would have the situation we have now.

Renew your mind, so that you may prove what is good and acceptable and the perfect will of God. In order for that to happen, there has to be a shift in our thinking. It's on us, the children of God, to develop that new mindset. The only way to change the old mindset is with the instructions from the Word of God.

That's the only way that a new mindset is going to spring up. It's not going to happen by our singing in the choir—we've tried that. It's not going to happen while we're working on the usher board; we've tried that too. It's not going to happen outside of the direct Word of God. And then it's on you, the student of the Word, to apply it. Trust me, if you sit under the Word long enough, you will get changed in your thinking. If you hang around God long enough, something will happen to you in the way you think.

We are trying to embody what is good and acceptable and perfect—the complete will of God. We all know that the will of God is the Word of God. This mindset helps us put on display what God wants to be seen and shown by our living out the Word of God, which puts believers on display.

Think about today for a moment. We have so many problems in our society, but when you boil them all down, everything traces back to an unhealthy mindset. The world is shouting, "Just be yourself, baby!" Okay. You're going to be yourself, and I'm going to be myself, and we are going to be crazy together. We will have exactly what we already have right now—chaos.

So, with that in mind, let's go to the book of Ephesians 4:17. As Paul writes to the church, he says, "This I say therefore, and testify in the Lord, that ye henceforth walk not as other Gentiles walk, in the vanity of their mind." He was talking to Gentiles who accepted Christ. As you know, a Gentile was anyone that was not Jewish. We have accepted Christ, right? And since we have accepted Him, there should be a visible difference in our lives when compared to the lives of folks who haven't. That's what the text is saying here. If you were to hold up a Christ-following Gentile next to an average Gentile, you'd be able to see, hear, and know the difference.

Now, how do you think that falls in the vanity of their mind? The phrase is referring to moral ineptness. Like it or not, we were raised to live immoral lives. For us, going to church was just that: going to church. It was never going to change anything, so we just saw it as another part of our schedule. We always heard, "You either go to church, or you die," but we never taught any deeper than that. Then, as a reward, we would listen to a preacher preaching fire and brimstone, but not instructing us in the Word.

Paul is saying that we should be living a life of virtue in the midst of moral decay. If you accept Christ, and if you understand the importance of studying scripture, there should be a noticeable change that takes place in your thinking. Everyone should be able to see it. I don't care if they are your sister, your best friend, your wife, or a complete stranger. That is why I need to clarify. If I have entered into the truth, and the person I'm with hasn't, I'm not going to sweat it. I'm not fussing at her. No, I'm going to work at growing this thing in my own life. And according to the Word, if people see the Word of God working in me and through me, they will be drawn to Jesus Christ.

Paul says that those who have not accepted Christ are walking in moral depravity. On the other side of that coin, those who have accepted Christ shouldn't be walking in moral depravity. Makes sense, right? The church has a mandate from God that says we are not to walk like those who are outside of Jesus Christ.

Paul describes the Gentiles that are outside of the church and tells us how to identify them. It's a vicious cycle. Moral depravity darkens your understanding of right or wrong. A little while ago, you didn't really care where you woke up or who you woke up with. You thought it was cool. But now, even the thought alone rubs you the wrong way. As a matter of fact, when someone mentions what we did in our past, our response may be, "I can't believe I did that!" You still have the capacity and the tools to make those same mistakes. But your mind has changed about that, so you don't participate anymore. It's not about the means, it's that your mindset towards moral depravity has changed.

Anything you enter into in this life requires a mindset change. Having babies requires a major one, right? They don't ask for your permission, either. You're going to change whether you want to or not. "I'm going to cry at 2 in the morning, so you are going to get your lazy self up and do something about it. I'm not going to tell you what I want, so you better keep trying stuff until you find out what it is. Now, I'm going to sleep for 15 minutes, but then you're going to get up and help me again. I don't care how much you fuss, or how much you cuss. You are going to learn to take care of me." And from the time they are born until they're 18 or so, just let them go. Go to school, go somewhere! You'll just want your mind back.

Anyway, back to Paul. He says that the Gentiles have darkened understanding because of the moral depravity of their mind. The ability to reason and understand what they're doing (and what it's doing to them) is absent. They're alienated from the life of God through sheer ignorance. The church has been in ignorance for so long. Sure, we've been coming to the building every week, but we're ignorant of how to serve God as He wants to be served and understanding what we can do as His children.

For years, we just clung to those old sayings. We try to let a song do what only the Word can do. We're shouting loud and claiming things in the name of the Holy Ghost when they have nothing to do with God. Walking in moral depravity darkens your understanding of right and wrong. It takes away from being God's child, but He's already paid the price for you. This ignorance has to do with a blindness in our hearts.

So many people like to defend themselves. "I wasn't that bad." That's like saying you were just a little bit blind. Does that make sense? You're either blind, or you can see. The church has to understand that darkening was never God's goal. The enemy wants to keep us in that darkness, but Peter says that we've been translated from darkness to light. He reminds us that we have been placed into the kingdom of God's own Son. I'm sure you understand that the darkness doesn't really go anywhere. Your mind just...changes. You need to change the way you think, and only then will you come out of darkness and move into the light.

Paul asserts that having clear understanding prevents being alienated from God by our inner ignorance. This ignorance in them is called their "old nature." When the old nature is in control, oblivious to what the new nature wants, we live in darkness, alienated from God by the blindness of our hearts. That's why we have to say, for any believer, a new mindset is essential.

Think of rituals and traditions. I've heard that it ain't a new year unless you cook some collard greens and black-eyed peas. My wife's grandmother said the reason she cooked collard greens on the first day of the year was because "you will have dollar bills all year long." She also said, "If you cook peas on the first day of the year, you will have only pennies." Now, we all know that's just some old wives' fable. Those kinds of things, to be honest with you, need to be eliminated from our mindset altogether. We shouldn't participate in them anymore. You may say it doesn't do any harm, but I know it does. It keeps ignorance in the front seat.

You see a black cat, so you turn around and go the other way. For what? You want to go all the way around the block just to avoid a black cat? You must know that the cat is trying to get out of your way. We have to move away from that kind of thinking. Those thoughts handicap us. If you throw some salt over your right shoulder, what's that going to do? It's just superstition, and it has no place here. We need to leave it behind.

You can't participate in superstition without an effect on your relationship with God. People used to tell me, "Make sure your house is clean on New Year's!" What if it's not? What if you are sick in bed and can't clean? The longer we participate, the longer we stand in darkness. All superstition, all things that support any kind of ignorance have to be eliminated from our mindset altogether.

We have to train ourselves not to even speak of things like that. As long as we talk about them, they are right here with us. We keep them alive with our words.

In the next verse, Paul says, "Who being past feeling have given themselves over unto lasciviousness, to work all uncleanness with greediness." Look at what is happening in the world today. Look at what people are doing, with no trace of remorse. So many people are not sorry for the wrong they've done, or even embarrassed others. They're past feeling entirely and have no shame or remorse.

The danger in that is obvious. Often, it's our feelings that prevent us from making right decisions or taking something too far. Paul tells us that those who are past feeling have given themselves over to all kinds of unrighteousness. They work all uncleanliness with greediness, in direct opposition to the will of God.

The internet's most profitable business is sexual pornography, and this, unfortunately, includes child pornography. Experts say that the internet makes billions of dollars a year in pornography alone. People say they want to stop it, but they really don't. Nobody wants to shut down an operation that makes that kind of money, especially not when they're getting a cut of the profits.

But because we are children of God, we know there must be a way to fight this. How can we introduce something to the internet that people will gravitate more towards instead of pornography? It would have to be something that is just as exciting, just as dramatic, and just as captivating, but morally clean. It wouldn't cause perversion; it would steer people away from it. God has to have something that is just as exciting.

Those who are past feelings give themselves over to unclean thoughts. This is what happens when you make an offering of yourself to sin. Once you do that, Satan is free to do whatever he wants with you and through you. Sometimes, even believers continue participating in the things they're supposed to be walking away from. They continue to engage in the exact sin from which they claim they've been delivered.

How do you make an offering of yourself to God instead? Basically, hand yourself over to Him. If you turn yourself over to your own self, that's a dangerous place to be. Me in my own hands? That's going to cause some problems. Those who are past feelings, do everything they desire to do, with greed perverting the whole process. They are going after it with a vengeance and an unquenchable desire. For the believer, there has to be a mindset to go after God with that same zeal. It's okay to be greedy for God because you can never get enough of Him. But the only result of worldly greediness is death, plain and simple.

In verse 20, Paul brings the discussion back to the believer. He says, "But ye have not so learned Christ." Look at verse 21: "If so be that ye have heard him, and have been taught by him, as the truth is in Jesus." Jesus is the truth. He is the way, and He is the light. Whenever you read about hearing in the Bible, it comes with the implication of putting what you hear into action.

A lot of us have heard, but with some of us, it's in one

ear and out the other. If you listened to the truth, you wouldn't smoke any more weed. If you paid attention to the truth, you would abandon sexual perversion. I made a decision to stop. You can't really hear the truth and keep doing the same thing you did before you heard it. Verse 22 says, "That ye put off concerning the former conversation the old man, which is corrupt according to the deceitful lusts."

We are always excusing ourselves. "I just can't stop!" What is it that you hear, then? Who is talking to you? "I just can't seem to stop. I keep going back." Really? Did you really hear? Were you really taught? If you listened to the truth and you didn't change, maybe you have a little more work to do. See, it's all in your mindset. We don't really believe we can stop anything we set our minds to. But if you got tired enough of something, you could stop it. We do it with people all the time, especially in the church.

You might say that this is your last time, but do you believe you have the ability to stop? Any counselor you talk to would first ask you, "Are you ready to quit?" The decision rests with you, not anyone else. If you are ready to quit, then stop.

Now that you are putting off concern for the old man, quit doing things the old man likes. Quit doing things he suggests. Even though you have been born of him, you aren't him anymore. Stop. God wouldn't ask you to do that unless He had something more powerful than the old man. In the hearing and the teaching, there's information passed along on how to quit doing this.

So if we really want to lay hold of what God has for us, we have to undergo a transformation of the mind. The one we have now won't cut it. First of all, you are in a new kingdom—the kingdom of light. You can't function in the kingdom of light when all of your thoughts are surrounded by darkness. And we are slowly finding out it doesn't happen overnight, especially when we are resistant to it.

You need to put aside your desires. You put off the old man because he's corrupt, led by deceitful lust. Those are strong words! Lust is deceitful, so we can't leave it unchecked. You think it's going to make you feel better and better, but it's just an empty vessel that will never be full. Paul is basically saying, "Believers in the church should be easily identified by the way they live compared to folks who aren't believers."

Did you know that, when the world talks about church people, they say that we're always saying one thing and doing another? "We don't talk to you Christians. You guys have more junk going on in the church than we ever could have out here. At least we attack somebody and move on. You all keep attacking the same person over and over again. You won't obey the pastor, but then when you go outside, you say we need to go to church? No, I don't. I plead the fifth on that." They say people in the church can't be trusted. They blab about everything with loose lips. But on the streets, talk is cheap.

We need to be renewed in the spirit of our minds. The entire transformation takes place right between your ears. That's where you struggle with doing what God says, and you wind up doing what you want to do instead.

When we are born again, it's our spirit that gets born

again, right? The Holy Spirit comes into our spirit and re-
lays information to our spirit. Then comes the hard part:
Our spirit has to relay that same information to our mind.
My mind isn't born again. My memories and thoughts
aren't born again. That goes away when I go away. But I
need my brain to get on board with what the Spirit is
telling me.

That's what Paul is talking about. A lot of us think our
fight is with our flesh. No, your hands aren't your problem—
your thoughts are. Your hands only do what your brain
says. We talk about our flesh like it's a separate entity, but
it's our mindset that must be changed if we want to carry
out the will of God in our lives. I have to get my mind
right. We were never taught that in church, though. We
made everything spiritual. But when I make up my mind to
follow Him, it's easy for the Spirit to use me.

There has to be a surrender of my mind to the Spirit. As
long as I rebel here, He can't do anything with me or
through me. My feet don't just walk to that girl's house on
their own accord. My feet didn't all of a sudden wake up
and say, "Okay, at 1:00 in the morning, we're headed to her
house." No, your brain said it, and you agreed. That's how
you ended up there. You could have easily said, "I'm not
going. It's just not right," and your brain would've had to
listen and obey.

No one can talk you into anything. You've already made
up your mind. They just come along to help you do what
you've already decided you'll do. Our culture today has
made us place so much value on friendship that we don't
think we can survive without friends. But God didn't talk

much about friends. He did tell us to have covenant brothers and sisters, though. What's the difference? Covenant brothers and sisters keep you in line.

If you're going to get drunk, I'm not going with you. I'm going to suggest that you don't go either. But true friends always understand. Covenant brothers and sisters know, deep down, that we should always do what God says.

Social media emphasizes this high price tag we place on friendships. How many friends do you have? I know all my covenant brothers. "I have 1,500 followers." Okay, but who do you really know? Who have you gone to lunch with and talked face to face with? Social media has tricked us into believing that we can't function without so-called "friends" in our circle or in our lives.

We bring that same idea to the church, though. I'm your pastor, but you want to be my friend? No, no, no. If I let you make me a friend, it's going to be hard to get you to do anything. That's why in the classroom, the teacher can't be your friend. You can't be in a position of authority and be a friend at the same time. We base everything on friendship. If our friend killed someone, we'd look the other way. "I ain't telling on my friend. I don't want to be a rat. I ain't no squealer." Really? Someone just got shot down, and you're going to pretend like it didn't happen?

For young people, their friends have more of an impact on them than I ever could. When I was growing up, I was always taught to never let anyone or anything come between me and my family. Nobody. If you're not my blood relative, I don't want to hear it. My family feeds me, clothes me, and houses me, so you sure aren't going to tell me to go against them, no matter how close of a friend you may be.

We grow up in ignorance, and we don't even notice it. It seems like the way to go. Why not? Everybody else is doing it. But when I meet Jesus, and I hear Him, and He teaches me the truth that is in Him, then I can finally change. That's why people say you act differently.

They'll ask, "How did you do that, dude?" You'd just tell them, "I made a choice. I met Jesus, and I made a choice. And the choice I made was that I didn't want to live like I was living anymore. It's available to you, too, but you have to be ready to make a choice. I'm not going to tell you that there aren't days when I struggle, but I've made a choice that I'm not going to take back. I accept the hard days, and He always gives me what I need to make it through them."

Sometimes you may say, "It's really hot. I sure could go for a cold beer. I just finished 12 straight hours of work, man. Toss me a cold one." The next thing you know, you're in line at Publix. "A cold bottle of beer would just be so nice right now. Nice and cool, just enough to buzz me." After a hard day's work crawling through ceilings, covered with sweat and dirt, water just doesn't hit the spot. You think about the taste of a cold brew at the end of a hot day, and it seems to make it all worthwhile.

But something on the inside of me rises up and says, "Hey! You decided to quit, remember? So, let's make water do what beer would do. Let's get a couple quarts of Gatorade and knock them back. We'll be okay."

A girl asks you, "Why don't you come over tonight? I'll

be ready at 10:00. You know where the key is." You're going to look in the closet and stare at those boxed-up shoes. But then that voice in you comes out and says, "Hey! You made a decision to stop. Now, let's go down to the kitchen, eat a sandwich, and let that idea pass away." Even married folks stare at the same shoes you do.

That's the reality we have to deal with. "Man, I sure would like to have a hit right now. I just feel like I need to be high. I know where I can go get some weed right now." Then, that voice rises up. "No! You made a choice. You made a decision that you were done." God says, "I want you to choose not to do it. Then, I can give you some power. But you don't want me to come in and do it for you, because you'll never grow up and beat it once and for all. You make the choice, and then I will come."

Every time you make the right decision, it gets easier and easier until it becomes second nature. Don't think you're going to do it one time and call it a day, though. This goes on for the rest of your life! When my time comes, I'll say, "Paul, thank you! The struggle is over. It's finally over."

But we don't have to go that way. We can just keep on doing what we've always done. The choice really is left up to us. It's not left up to God, even though we wish it was. This is not a group decision, either. It's going to have to take place in each individual's mind, and that will shape what they become.

2

~✦~

THE BLESSING OF A HUMBLE MINDSET

James 4:6-8

These are difficult and different times, especially for those who want to hand their social security check to someone at the bank and deposit it. Those days are pretty much dead and gone, but some of us have grown stubborn with age and refuse to change.

We carry around these cell phones that can do all kinds of crazy things, but all we want to do is make a call. I was in the cell phone store the other day, and a salesperson told me that the technology of the flip phone is going to be thrown out the window in about four months. That old phone won't be any good anymore because that technology costs the phone companies too much to maintain. Nowadays, you're either going to get a smartphone or no phone at all.

The smartphone is for the person who likes to have every little thing they do at their fingertips: email, texting, adding, subtracting, access to the internet, access to files, and so on. In fact, it seems like most of the business that takes place today is done that way. That's why you see people at lunch staring at their phones. Having all of that power in your pocket makes it very easy to communicate with other people and get things done wherever you are.

Schools are moving forward at that same pace. It won't be long now before your child just has to bring his tablet or phone to school to access learning. That's it. Basically, any textbook that they'll need is downloadable. Nobody buys physical textbooks anymore. Why would they? It's all on-line. Even when I'm teaching, I do video presentations. Any book I want to access is a Google search away. You can carry a hundred pounds of books on your hard drive. And you already know that a downloaded book is a lot cheaper than one that's printed on paper.

But adapting to all of these rapid changes requires a serious mindset shift. And for those of us who want to be involved in anything happening in the world today, be it financial, educational, or recreational, our mind has to adapt in order to participate. Since society has moved into video mode, teachers and coaches have to be innovative in order to reach people through what they *see* rather than what they *hear*.

Many people have been edged out of this economy not because they can't change their mind, but because they don't want to. You have to be very careful not to allow yourself to get stuck in one mindset and refuse to move on. The next era is going to happen with or without you, so you might as well get with the program. This is even true with God. He is so progressive, even though we want to make Him stagnant. He is always trying to move us to the next plateau, to the next rung of faith, to the next activity... but we get comfortable and stubborn. We think, "I just want to stay like this forever."

It's our responsibility to do the internal work to keep your mindset from becoming complacent. You have to fight for it. Change requires us to change, and we can't be timid in the face of the unfamiliar.

We all like to surround ourselves with things we can control, right? That way, we don't have to think when we interact with our environment or do whatever we need to do. It's just automatic, and we like it that way. We play it safe on purpose, even if it means we're worse off for it.

Well, I'm here to tell you that you're serving the wrong God. Everyone that God deals with gets yanked out of their comfort zone. When Moses went to Egypt, he had to lead people out of Egypt. God said, "Don't worry about it, just lead them." He is going to lead you in the same way, and you won't have to have what you think you'll need to just lead them.

You can't see where you're headed, but God tells you to go anyway, the odds are that our thinking will be like the children of Israel, "Man, I should have stayed where I was. At least I had water. At least I had food to eat." But every situation we come across and every move we make require a mindset change. If you want the next promotion, you have to change. You don't get promoted without taking on added responsibility. People say, "I would take the job, but I just don't want any more responsibility right now." That works...if you want to stay right where you are: unpromotable and broke.

Others say, "I just wish I had a lot of money." Even a windfall of money requires a serious mindset change. You can't manage a million dollars with a $10 mentality. One day, a friend of mine wanted to buy a Mercedes Benz. He went to the dealership and checked out a two-seater, 500 SEC, a real nice ride. But then he approached a sales rep and asked, "How much gas mileage does this get? What's the maintenance schedule like?"

The salesman looked him right in the eye and said, "I'll be honest with you, man. The people who buy this car don't ask those kinds of questions." You just don't go into a Mercedes dealership to buy a Benz if you are worried about maintenance and gas mileage.

That's us sometimes, though. We refuse to make the necessary changes, or we refuse to prepare for the changes on the front end, only to have to face them on the back end. That work needs to get done either way, so we might as well take care of it ahead of time. We really need to co-operate with God. We need to mold our mindset as He moves us. You might not realize it, but God is powerless to change your mindset. Unfortunately for us, that is our responsibility, and it's completely under our control.

I want to look at something that God asks of us on a regular basis: humility. People think being humble looks like getting down on your knees, but that's just a physical position. You could still be rebelling in your thoughts. When you see someone kneeling, you might say they're humble, but they really just switched positions. If you were truly humble, you could say that prayer in any position.

It's like when a mother asks a child to do something, and they do it, but they're complaining and griping in their mind the whole time. That's not humility at all. Some parents might say, "Hey, I'm just glad they did it." The truth is, though, that it's not benefiting anyone. At their core, they are still in rebellion in their thoughts.

When God tells you to be humble, He's not asking you to take on a different *physical* position. He's actually asking you to assume a different *mental* position. If you do that, then He can do something with you that would eventually be revealed physically. You've just got the order of operations wrong.

A good way to make sure there is humility in our mindset is to understand what the opposite of humility looks like—arrogance. Every chance you get, give God the glory and credit for what is happening in your life. Keep that up, and one day, your first thought when you wake up in the morning will be, "Thank You, Jesus!" We have to make sure we keep an eye on our arrogance because there's a tiny part of us that wants to take credit for every little thing around us. We might think, "That happened because of me. I'm smart, and I worked hard, and I didn't get any help from anyone." We forget how important humility is and how a humble mindset can benefit us in all sorts of ways.

However, you have to be really careful. As a believer, a humble mindset is a requirement if you're going to follow and interact with God. But God doesn't have a humble mindset—Jesus does. God is just as arrogant as can be. "Where were you when I formed everything? Where were you when I created existence?" He can be just as arrogant as He wants to be, but it's not arrogance because He's just stating fact. When Jesus came, He is the example of humility.

Turn with me to James 4:1-8. James is writing to a group of believers that were always striving to do a lot of things, which is what many of us do today, so let's try to view this text with that in mind. In this passage, he gives them the tools to understand the benefits of a humble mindset. We have all heard God say, "Humble yourself under the mighty hand of God that He may exalt you." So, the person who acknowledges God and gives Him the credit and the glory for everything that happens is someone whom God can elevate.

Many times, we are not elevated because our arrogance stops God from promoting us. We just won't give Him credit. And if you don't give God the credit, you take it for yourself.

In the first verse, he says, "From whence come wars and fightings among you?" This sounds like America, doesn't it? He goes on, "come they not hence, even of your lusts that war in your members?" When James talks about lusts, he's referring to all the things those believers are striving for. Next verse:

> Ye *lust and have not: ye kill and desire to have, and cannot obtain: ye fight and war, yet ye have not, because ye ask not.*

See what God's saying? "You're busy trying to gain all of that nonsense, but you're My people, and you're trying to make it happen all by yourself!" Everybody in the world preaches to pull yourself up by your own bootstraps. Make things happen for yourself. Do it for yourself, by yourself. But that doesn't work when you are a child of God.

Next verse: He says, "Ye ask, and receive not, because ye ask amiss." You don't get what you're asking for because, even if you're asking for the right thing, you want it for the wrong reason. You pretend as if you want money to pay the rent, but it may be to buy new shoes. There's a dishonesty in that. You're craving something that won't benefit the kingdom. If God gives it to you, you'll just consume it according to your own will instead of using it for the kingdom's agenda. James goes on.

Ye adulterers and adulteresses, know ye not that the friendship of the world is enmity with God? whosoever therefore will be a friend of the world is the enemy of God. Do ye think that the scripture saith in vain, the spirit that dwelleth in us lusteth to envy?

We see the parallels in our own situation. In America, we want everything we want, when we want it, and for ourselves. Even the church wants every member, and they want them for themselves. There's never a kingdom attachment to what we want, and yet we ask the God of the kingdom to bless us with it so that we can have it.

In verse 6, James contrasts the people in verses 1 through 5. They're struggling and striving to obtain these things and can't get them, but they are people of God. In verse 6, he shows you what it looks like for the people of God that have a different mindset. He says,

But he giveth more grace. Wherefore he saith, God re-sisteth the proud, but giveth grace unto the humble. Submit yourselves therefore to God. Resist the devil, and he will flee from you. Draw nigh to God, and he will draw nigh to you. Cleanse your hands, ye sinners; and purify your hearts, ye double-minded.

Just for a few minutes, let's discuss the benefits of a humble mindset. Grace can be defined as a number of things, but in this text, it has to do with recognition. In other words, God gives more recognition to the person with the humble mindset than the person with a proud mindset, especially when their pride is based on themselves instead of rooted in Him. It's almost like a proud mentality makes you invisible to God, and who on earth wants that?

The person with a humble mentality is very much visible to God because they're not only convinced that God is operating in their lives, but they rely on God to do so. And by being humble, they give God the freedom to get in there and make moves.

Humility makes us more visible. The person that has the humble mindset moves to the head of the class, and God recognizes that person, but He resists the proud. You have to be really careful. Arrogance and humility are separated by a fine line. It's easy to be arrogant and feel like you're being humble. It may sound like you're bragging about God, but you're actually just bragging about yourself.

Arrogance has a way of showing up in everything you do—even in your walk. You walk as if you are under the power of yourself, talking to people as if it's your power that gives you the ability to do what you do. Being humble doesn't mean groveling before God. It means that you acknowledge Him, not only for keeping you afloat but also for His constant blessings and provision.

That's an excellent way to maintain a mindset of humility. I have what I have because He allows me to have it. I do what I do because He lets me. It's His power, and He could snatch it away any time He wants. I really don't have any power apart from God. He loans it to me so I can do His will. When I do the opposite of His will, that's arrogance. When I choose to carry out His will over mine, that's humility.

James tells us that God resists the proud and gives grace to the humble. Humility is a state of mind, and Paul outlines it best when he talks about Jesus. He says, "Let this mind be in you, which was also in Christ Jesus." You have to be willing to let the mindset of God call the shots for you. He isn't saying you're equal with God, but he is praising the mindset of Jesus. Jesus knew that, even though He was fully God, putting God before Himself would not result in loss.

And to be real, none of us want to be less. We only act like that in church. Do you go to your job to be less? When you go to work and they tell you what to do, you do the best you can with that direction. Humility isn't physical; it's mental. The state of my mind must transform from independence to unashamed dependence on God. When I remove myself from the equation, God can use me.

Now, if I bow because I have a humble mindset,

bowing is good. But if I bow just for the sake of bowing, and then I'm still rebelling in my thought process, all I've done is change my physical position from standing up straight to bowing down.

What has to take place in the believer's life that makes this deep, internal humility possible? There's a word in the text that's going to rub all of us the wrong way, so prepare for it. While God gives grace to the humble, He sets himself in opposition to the proud.

Do you know why God really didn't like Pharaoh? He was too arrogant. That arrogance is revealed when he refused to do what Moses told him God needed him to do. "I ain't doing it. I'm Pharaoh. I don't know your God, and I don't know you, so I'm not letting Israel go." Then God sets Himself in opposition to Pharaoh, which is really neat because Pharaoh is the king of the entire world. Back then, Egypt was the entire world. Now you have the king of the entire world and the God of the entire universe going head to head because of Pharaoh's arrogance. God is thinking, "How dare you? You don't really know the One you are dealing with, but you will." So He set Himself in opposition, and you know the rest of the story.

I don't know about you, but I don't want God to be in opposition to me. How can we begin to purge the arrogance from our minds? First, you must submit yourself to God. Since God resists the proud and gives grace to the humble, you need to submit yourself to the God that can set Himself in opposition against you.

Again, submission to God is not one-fold. Many believers think that they can simply submit to God without submitting to anything else. You have to understand that when you submit to Him, you're also submitting to His Word and His Spirit because they're all one package.

The very nature of being submissive to anything is admitting its authority over you. You submit yourself to the authority of the manager that supervises you at work. You submit yourself to the authority of the man you marry. For so many of us, humility just means kneeling down, which is nothing but a change in position. To attempt to submit to God only without submitting to the whole kingdom of God is misguided at best.

Many people don't like the police nowadays. Did you know that God established the police? The police force is a major part of the order that God has set up in your city. God wants us to obey the authority that He has appointed. You may think, "I don't like the police. Even the sight of one of their uniforms makes me sick to my stomach." How are you going to surrender to God without honoring the organization that He has established?

Children, how do you submit to your heavenly Father and not to your earthly father and mother? How do you go to school in the morning and then refuse to submit to your teachers in the afternoon? Every teacher is an authority figure. It doesn't matter whether or not you like them. You are not sent to like—you are sent to obey. That's the problem we have with everything. We don't obey because we don't like the authority.

When you humble yourself to God, you can finally take

a stand against the enemy. That may sound absolutely nuts to us. We say things like, "I would submit to my boss if he didn't make it so impossible for me to do so." Really? We have to work that out, don't we? How can I claim that I submit to God and disrespect my boss? I can't.

Everyone's boss sits in a position of a God-permitted authority. I must recognize that my humility is going to be challenged, especially in our society. Being humble doesn't make you a doormat. If you really look at the gospel, Jesus was anything but a doormat. He knew how to take a stand because He relied on God and the Word of God that was made available to Him above all else. He wasn't anybody's doormat. If I'm responding with humility to what God has made available to me, I don't have to worry about what you say or do. God will take care of you and make sure you don't stop me from going where I need to go.

The reason we can't catch onto this is our undying arrogance won't let us keep our mouth shut. A lot of us can't get promoted because we flap our lips too much, and we spend all our time with people who do the exact same thing. Most of the people you work with complain about their job and don't even actually do it. If they really did their job, they wouldn't have time to complain. They are so busy fussing and griping about this and that. But if you were to suggest that they quit, they'd say, "Quit? No, I can't quit!" Then shut up. You can't do both. You've either got to shut up and work or quit and leave—one of the two. And many of us act the exact same way. They feel comfortable in our presence talking that way because we don't demonstrate a different character in their presence.

If you want to have a humble mindset, you are going to submit to one of two entities. You can either submit to God or the devil. And if you don't submit to God, you'll automatically submit to the devil, whether you want to or not.

When we submit to God, we align ourselves with Him. We place ourselves in a position of order under the authority of the word of God. Sometimes, this feels especially hard because we haven't seen God or Jesus either. We just read about Him in the scriptures. God knows we can't see Him standing right in front of us.

You can picture Him saying, "You haven't seen Me before, and you never will. And as if that isn't enough, you won't see my Son until judgment day. Those that did see Him, they've been dead for ages. But you can, by faith, surrender yourself or subject yourself to My Word, and I will honor that as you submitting to My Son and I. Then, you and I will be good as gold. Now, if I held you responsible for being submissive to My Son directly, I know you could never achieve it because He's sitting right next to Me. But since He and I and the Spirit are one, I acknowledge that anyone who submits to My Word is actually submitting to all of us."

We make it hard, but it's really simple. All this means is that the Word of God becomes the authority in my everyday life. Regardless of what anybody else says or does, I make the decision that the Word of God starts and stops with me.

Humility is not negotiable, although many parents negotiate humility. "Just do what I say. I don't care how you feel, just do it." I read a book about disciplining children, and it said that discipline doesn't stop until you hear humility in the voice of the child. If you don't hear humility in the child's voice, then it's not present at all. And when humility is absent, arrogance and pride are right there, even if they do exactly what you say.

Despite what you may think, there's no humility in coming to church. People show up just as proud as can be. Do you actually know where humility comes in? Being the church. If it comes down to being the church, I'm no longer independent. The arrogant person will never be able to go toe to toe with Satan and win. Your pride will never win that battle.

Samuel told Saul, "This is the order from God. When you fight the Ammonites, kill everybody. Kill the king, kill the queen, kill the soldiers... Kill everybody. Boys, girls. Kill all the animals. Kill every last one of them." He says, "Yes, sir. Got it." Then, when he goes down into the battle, he makes a different decision. Arrogance invades. He decides, "I'm going to keep the king alive. I may need him to negotiate some kind of deal with another nation." We already know that wasn't what God asked of him. A decision like that doesn't seem like it would hurt anything, and I guess it really didn't in the long run.

What Saul did wasn't powerful enough to foil God's plan because God doesn't bow to disobedience. The only thing it really did was stop Saul from being actively involved with God's plan. Sometimes you may think you're with God, but He'll say, "You're too arrogant! You don't need me. Go and do your thing. You doing your thing will not interrupt Me doing My thing. That's what every arrogant person needs to know. You can be as arrogant as you want and as prideful as you want, and I don't have to worry about you. You're not going to have any victories to celebrate anyway. The devil is going to kick your butt every time because you actually think that you could go up against him by yourself and win."

So, Saul disobeyed. And here's where it gets dangerous: Pride and arrogance make the person who is prideful and arrogant believe they hear from God. When Samuel showed up, the first thing he noticed was that the sheep and goats were making noise.

So he asked, "What's going on? Why do I hear sheep and goats? Didn't you do what I said?"

And Saul replied, "Yes, I did."

Samuel must have said, "Well, somebody is crazy today. I see kings and goats and sheep alive and well. What's the deal?"

Now, watch how Saul responded, which is exactly how prideful people react when you confront them. "I looked at the sheep and the goats, and I decided that they look good enough to sacrifice to God."

Samuel said, "Wow. Really? I could have sworn that your orders were to kill them."

And Saul won't give up: "Yeah, okay. But I was thinking, wouldn't it be great if I just kept these animals alive? That way, we would always have animals to sacrifice to God."

That's a real arrogant decision, even though it might look like serving God in our own eyes. It's totally backwards. Think about it. It's shouting, "I'm going to disobey, and then use what I disobey with as an offering to God, who requires my obedience." Arrogance makes you absolutely crazy.

If your pastor gives you an order to do something, and you don't do precisely what he says, will it upset the balance of things? Not really. It's just that you won't be included in his future plans because he knows that you can't carry out simple orders.

It should be no surprise that Saul was immediately dismissed from the throne. Samuel said, "God has had it with you! Right now, the kingdom of Israel is stripped from you." Saul was standing there with his crown on, but we all know that it was never about the crown. It's always about the anointing of the Holy Spirit, and the Spirit being able to operate in the life of the one who is humble. When any person is prideful and arrogant, he ceases to serve his purpose, which makes it awfully hard for God to use him at all.

In Ephesians 4:27, Paul is basically telling the church, "Don't make room in your mind or in your life for the devil. Don't give him any place, because he's greedy. He doesn't just want that little slice, he wants it all."

God says that arrogance gets in the way. Did that stop God from sending Jesus? No. Did that prevent God from giving us all His promises? No, it just means that you won't be included in His plan. God kicked Satan out in the first place because Satan was as arrogant as they come. So be as arrogant as you want. The only thing it will do is cut you out of God's plan. And you can't get back into the plan until you fix the arrogant mindset that got you booted out in the first place.

"Draw nigh to God and He will draw nigh to you." But since we can't see God, there's no physical movement towards Him. But there is a mental posture, a state of being, that pulls us close to Him and Him close to us. When I live humbly, I invite His presence in. When I live in arrogance, His presence grieves.

For a long time, the church never equated how we live with our association with God. We figure that, because we come to church on Sunday, we did our part, and that's that.

How are we supposed to draw close to Him? The first thing we have to do is cleanse our hands. This is a metaphor, of course, that means we shouldn't participate in unrighteousness. We like to deflect the blame and say, "They talked me into it. I didn't even want to try, but everyone else wanted me to, and they convinced me." Refusing to participate in unrighteousness is a choice that the believer makes because they have decided, "I want a closer relationship with God. And in order to have that, I have to remove myself from unrighteous activity. I need to develop a righteous mindset."

None of us like the term, "sinner." If you're involved in unrighteous activity, someone might categorize you based on what you're doing. For example, if you eat a lot of ice cream (an abnormal amount of ice cream), you'll probably earn a nickname that has something to do with that. It's hard to ignore. People call you things based on what they see. The fact is, if we involve ourselves with sin, the term for us would technically be "sinners."

James 4 is saying, "Cleanse your hands, you sinners. Purify your heart and your mind." He's talking about cleaning up the way we think and make decisions. Our thought process is the sum total of what we read, what we hear, and what we see. We have to be careful about what we take in because it has such a dramatic effect on what we put out.

James doesn't say that the power of God will come upon you to make this happen. James doesn't say that if you just pray to God, the Spirit will go and find you a new mind, then take your old mind out and put the new one in. That's what we used to pray. "Remove my old nature. Remove my old mind and give me a new one." And then we prayed, "God, if you find any wickedness in me, snatch it out." But unfortunately, many of us are not being truthful with ourselves. We don't really mean that. If God started examining things and pulling stuff out, we would have great discomfort. We are uncomfortable now with the changes the Holy Spirit wants to make in our lives.

Then James refers to people like that as double-minded. In this text, it has to do with being unstable in the way of having misplaced loyalty. Anyone who is double-minded is trying to serve two masters, whether he knows it or not. His loyalty isn't actually to the God of heaven, although he wants it to be so, and he thinks it is because he's doing certain things that appear to be godly.

But his/her loyalty IS NOT TO God. He/she is involved in things that are not righteous, and he/she hasn't cleansed his/her mind or embraced a mindset of humility. In other words, he/she is trying to straddle the fence, and you can only do that for so long before you fall off.

When you grow up in church, you want to run off as you get a little older. We always believe that the grass is greener on the other side. You know why we always think like that in the church? Because people seldom tell us the truth about the grass on the other side. Almost never.

Everyone's always talking about their relationship with God like it's been picture perfect throughout their entire life. My testimony includes that I'm still going through stuff. I'm still learning, and the places I've been are very unpleasant. We always talk about our relationship with God as if we've always been saved, causing the person out there who is struggling to think there's no hope for them. You want people to believe you've always been exactly like you are now. Unfortunately, that arrogance actually keeps people from the church.

We should be saying, "Yeah, I was on the other side of the fence. I ate all kinds of grass over there. And what I didn't eat, I smoked!" We can't keep up this charade. It's all just arrogance, and we need to drop it. If we tell the truth and let humility lead the way, we can really start impacting lives.

We should want people to know we were on the other side of the fence, then others would know there's hope for them too. Whenever you come off like you're some saint that's never said a curse word or done anything wrong, people think there's no hope for them because they are still knee-deep in moral depravity.

Arrogance makes us want to appear better than we really are. Have you ever listened to someone's testimony and thought, "Based on what you're telling me, it sounds like you never needed saving in the first place! My record is 100 times worse than that. I'm surprised God even looked at it. I might as well go and ride sin all the way to hell because I never even have a chance."

Have you never made any mistakes? Have you accomplished everything you ever set your mind to do? No failures? No lessons? You must be lying. Everyone trips and falls. Inflating yourself like that just shows that you don't know the power of a true testimony. Humility shines the light of glory back on God and highlights everything He's done for you. That's what inspires and encourages, not some perfect robot.

If you're planning on sharing your testimony without including all the hard parts, don't even bother. Did you spend half your life in jail? Tell them! Did you spend your college years in rebellion? Tell them! Tell them how you submitted, and how your life has changed because of God's grace and mercy.

We need to remind people that they're not too far gone. They can still rise up out of whatever foolishness they're in right now. We need to say to them, "I used to be just like you, but God made me new. I still struggle all the time, but I'm better. If He reached down and touched my heart, I know He'd do the same for you and then some."

A humble person isn't interested in making himself look better than the person he's talking to. He's actually interested in the person finding and trusting God. This takes him out of the picture and puts God front and center. God gives more grace and recognition to the humble—it's that simple. This idea of submission brings us into an agreement with God in which we draw closer to Him, and He does the same to us.

That's where He wants us: close to Him. The idea of closeness has to do with oneness. When I'm close to Him, He can work through me. When I'm close to Him, He can use me. When I'm close to Him, His thoughts and His ways become my own. Our wants and desires merge. He can do whatever He desires through me, except push me away.

Of course, Jesus gives us the perfect example. "Let this mind be in you which is also in Christ Jesus." We might be tempted to think, "Now, you know if I went through the trouble of coming all the way down here from heaven, I'd at least make myself the king of some country. I'm not coming to earth to be a carpenter or walk around on the streets. I'm not going to take some low-paying job without benefits or retirement." But He made Himself humble of no reputation. Jesus' mindset was, "I will lay down if it means that it will exalt God."

I'm not here to judge whether someone is doing things the right way or the wrong way. My job is to be humble and submit to the role God has given me to play. That's why church members are difficult for pastors to deal with. They have to resist what they want to do and work within the vision that God has given the pastor. It's difficult to be cool with that which you can't see!

When you rebel against authority through arrogance, you don't ruin God's plans—you just remove yourself from them. The kingdom doesn't need you.

Humble yourselves, therefore, under the mighty hand of God that he may exalt you in due time (1 Peter 5:6).

Expect it, and get excited about it!

3

PUTTING ON A NEW MINDSET

Romans 12:2

We never really know how much damage we're subjected to on a regular basis until we have to undergo a mind transformation. We never truly understand the impact of how we were raised, the people we grew up around, the instructions we were given, and how men taught other men to be men and women taught other women to be women. When we come to Christ, we discover that none of the information we were given was accurate. But the problem is that all of the information is cemented into our makeup now. It has made us who we are today.

How am I supposed to transform my thinking and become a new person if everything I think is filtered through my old lens? The good news is scripture tells us how we can develop a new mindset in the light of who we already are. Every endeavor we embark on, every job we have, every promotion we get is going to require that we change our mindset. We can't perform at a higher level with the same mindset we had at a lower level. Something has to change, and that something is sitting right between our ears.

A lot of people have a problem with that, so don't worry; you're not alone. If a successful person wants to have a relationship with unsuccessful people, a different mindset is required unless he or she is trying to help them. Why? Because unsuccessful people believe that they are alright where they are. Successful people will eventually alter their mindset or thinking to cater to the mindset of unsuccessful people. If you have to stoop down and backpedal to spend time with your inner circle, then you are living backwards. And who wants that? You need to focus on what's ahead.

The problem is that people will do almost anything to avoid having to change their minds about the way they live. They want what they want, how they want it, and when they want it, but they don't want anything said to them. Let's be real, though. If we actually went around doing everything we felt like doing and listening to that deprived side of us, we'd all end up in jail or six feet under.

We have to make sure we know how to change our minds. It doesn't matter if you're in the church or outside of it, either. Think about transitioning from adolescence to adulthood. You can't still be a boy and try to operate as a man. If you do that, you'll make a mess of it every time. Before a boy can really become a man, the boy in him has to totally die off.

Paul says in Romans 12 that we shouldn't allow ourselves to be fashioned according to the pattern of this world. This place is full to the brim with the lust of the flesh. He doesn't just tell us not to be *conformed*, he instructs us to be *transformed*. You can't just do the first part. You have to go in 100% on both halves of what Paul is saying.

See, even though we're not in heaven just yet, we're

meant to move and grow in that direction. We're meant to take part in the renovation of our patterns of thought. We already know what it takes to develop an unhealthy mindset: just do what we've always done and what everyone around us is already doing.

In Ephesians 4:23, Paul is talking to the church of believers at Ephesus who, according to the introduction, are rich beyond measure. The problem is that they're living like people who are broke—spiritually bankrupt. He says, "And be renewed in the spirit of your mind."

Now, the word "renewed" in this passage doesn't have the exact same meaning as its usage in Romans 12. In Ephesians, Paul is specifically referring to spiritual vitality. Remember, these believers were not living up to the standard that God had set for them. God showered them with blessings, but they were still living like they were flat broke.

Imagine being so run-down and fatigued that you might as well be knocking on death's door. When you feel that way, you run to the doctor's office and get a B12 shot, and that's supposed to revitalize your immune system. With that immunity boost, your body will be able to fight off germs and prevent you from catching colds and the flu. Paul is saying that these believers need a spiritual B12 shot to revitalize their spirituality.

In verse 24, Paul discusses putting on the new man. We've looked at the old man, and now it's time to upgrade. It sounds like he's saying that you need to change clothes. You need to take off those ratty old rags and put on a nice, pressed suit. When you do that, you'll feel sharp as a tack, ready to take on the world.

The full verse is, "And that ye put on the new man, which after God is created in righteousness and true holiness." Why is the new man so important? Because the new man is fashioned after God, and the old one is fashioned after the pattern of this world. Big difference, right? You might be wondering if the new man is the Holy Spirit, but we'll get there in a moment.

When I was a kid, playing cowboys and Indians was all we did. Every Christmas, in my neighborhood, you got a cowboy hat, two of those cap pistols, those things that cover your legs when you're roping cattle, and one of those little stick horses. It had a stuffed horse head, but really, it was just a broom handle. To us, though, it really didn't matter, because we were able to use our imagination. We'd be bucking around waving those cap guns in the air. When we dressed like a cowboy, we began to act like one.

Romans 6:3 says,

Know ye not, that so many of us as were baptized into Jesus Christ were baptized into his death? Therefore we are buried with him by baptism into death: that like as Christ was raised up from the dead by the glory of the Father, even so we also should walk in newness of life.

When you accepted Christ as your personal Savior, you accepted the death of Christ as well. When a person gets baptized as a new believer, that water baptism is synonymous with dying. In this sense, God requires us to copy the way Jesus walked in newness.

He's not asking us to copy Paul or Moses, but Jesus Himself to identify with Christ. That's the new man. For simplicity's sake, let's just say that the new identity we want is the identity of Jesus Christ. That's the identity that will allow us to test God's Word and find out if it really works.

The question, then, becomes this: What practical steps can we take right now to move towards that complete renewal? Well, I've learned that anything can be changed in two weeks if you really want to do something about it. Something that took you 40 years to learn can be uninstalled in two weeks but only if you consistently do the opposite of what you have learned.

I used to despise cauliflower. My mom would cook it all the time. It has a bland taste, and even when you cover it with salt, that bland flavor still ruins every bite. We were supposed to eat it raw because apparently, that's the best way to eat it. That lady kept feeding me cauliflower until I developed a liking for it. As you can imagine, that made me a firm believer in this principle. If you are dying to make a change, purposely do the exact opposite of what you've always done. If you keep on doing the same old thing, it'll only strengthen the bad habit's stronghold on your mind.

God warns us about things like fornication and pornography because they can grab us and control our thinking. We are surrounded by people who have no control over their own thoughts—it's actually the other way around. Whatever pops into their mind makes their decisions for them. They have no self-control. What those poor souls don't know is that they can turn that right around if they consistently choose to do the opposite of what their thoughts tell them to do.

You know that I learned to like cauliflower, but did you know that I couldn't stand Brussels sprouts either? My mama kept feeding them to me, and now I don't sweat them. I don't think there's any type of food that I don't like, because that woman fed me everything. When you grow up in a house with seven children, nobody has a choice in what they eat. She would put dinner on the table, and if anybody said, "I don't like that. I don't want it," she'd say, "Well, let me tell you something. When I close that kitchen down, it's gonna be closed until morning." That's how my sister learned to eat collard greens.

Every little thing that we need to do in order to develop a new mindset is not listed in these few verses. Still, they give us an idea of the direction we need to grow in if we really want to change for the better.

Last time I checked, the local high school only had a 50% graduation rate. That is so wild to me. You're telling me that only half of the kids who show up for class on the first day of 9th grade will get a diploma? Some drop out, some go to jail, some get pregnant, and some just wind up spending time with the wrong people and end up in the wrong place at the wrong time.

Some people don't see anything wrong with dropping out of high school, though. That's their mindset. "I can just go work at Walmart instead of sitting through class all day. That way, I'll actually make some money." That might work for a young kid, but what about when you get a little older? You'll need to make more than $8 an hour at some point unless you're planning on living with your mama for the rest of your life.

That mindset starts there, but it can drive you to other things in your life because of where your priorities are and the way you think and make decisions. You might start selling dope. Why? You say, "Because everybody needs money, right? And what else am I supposed to do? The reality is that I quit school. Nobody is going to hire me without a high school diploma. If I actually manage to land a job, I'm only going to make $8 an hour. That isn't enough! I have way too much to pay for. The only thing left for me is selling dope. I can make cash fast." You will not understand the impact of that choice when you make it. Things like that drag us further down, but we are fooled into thinking that the money is pulling us back up.

Let's go to Ephesians 4:25, which says, "Wherefore putting away lying, speak every man truth with his neighbor: for we are members one of another." You might be wondering how anyone is supposed to turn on a dime like that. If you constantly lie, now is the time to change. Every time your mouth starts to lie, you correct it and tell the truth. After two straight weeks of telling the truth, you might just stop lying altogether. If you practice that in every conversation you have, your whole vocabulary will shift.

Despite what you may like to think, telling people a lie instead of the truth doesn't help them one bit. Paul maintains that when a believer purposely lies to another believer, it not only hurts the believer that's being lied to, it hurts the one that's lying. I know we want the world to believe we don't struggle with anything, and sometimes it's easier to just sweep it under the rug, but let's be real. Let's be truthful. You're not protecting anyone with that lie—not even yourself.

Here's the hard part: If someone comes to me with an issue, I shouldn't spare their feelings by lying. I should love him enough to tell him the truth because at least the truth can actually do something for him. I'll never know when I might need that neighbor to help me. We want to make sure we don't hurt anyone's feelings, but when we lie, we hurt them much more deeply than an honest opinion ever could. We keep them in the dark, and they have no way of knowing that.

Just keep an eye on it for two weeks and correct yourself as soon as you hear a lie bubble up within you, even a tiny one. I guarantee you'll see a difference.

Paul says we are members of one another. The body of Christ is made up of many, many, many people, but we all need each other. It's kind of like football. You know what really turns me off about football today, though? I like to watch the game, but the pro level has way too many individual celebrations. It's over the top now. Say, your team is losing 30 to nothing, and you score a touchdown, so you hop and skip and jump around? Your team is still losing. If you're celebrating your own victory over the team's, you're not a team player. Football is supposed to be a team sport. Today in the NFL and the college ranks, coaches are having so much difficulty with young men who don't know how to play as a unit. "It's all about my stats, man. Yeah, we lost, but I don't care. I got my stats up."

If you're so concerned with your own self, maybe you

should play a solo sport, like golf. Football is supposed to be about the people around you, not just you. Whenever we get a new job, we must learn to be team players, but our mindset keeps us from doing that. We have to learn how to flip this thing around so that we can act like one body. We are members of one another.

In Ephesians 4:26, Paul says, "Be ye angry, and sin not: let not the sun go down upon your wrath." He knows that everyone gets angry at times, but he's warning us against allowing that anger to lay hold of our mindsets and cause us to behave inappropriately. When someone badmouths you, you might want to knock them out, but isn't it better to walk away and let that dust settle instead?

Here's a thought that might help you: When people talk about me, I already know they're lying. They don't know enough about me to tell the truth. So why should I get angry when someone is talking about me if they have no idea who I really am? All they're doing is saying what they think or believe about me, and that doesn't mean it's true.

We shouldn't even waste time chasing after them, trying to make them take back what they said when it was a lie anyway. No need to take it that seriously. Paul is basically saying, "I'm not demanding that you never get angry. I'm just telling you that you can't let anger cause you to sin."

When believers sinned in the Old Testament, it meant that they violated the law, and that was reason enough to stone them to death. In the New Testament, when you sin, you're narrowing the scope of what God has for you. When I allow my anger to make decisions for me, and I behave in a way that disrespects God and His Word, it pulls me further from His hands.

Paul is telling us not to let the sun set on our anger. When you sleep on something that's frustrating you, you're just eight hours angrier in the morning. Nothing magically disappears. You need to settle that thing with whomever is concerned before your head hits the pillow, because the moment you lay down, the enemy is on his way. He's coming to plant seeds of anger until you finally make up your mind: "The next time I see him, I'm going to punch him square in the face." That's basically what we have in the streets today. People are angry, but they don't know how to control or deal with their anger. And when it goes unresolved, they take it out on whoever made them angry. But we all know that anger is not the fruit of the Holy Spirit.

Let's look at Ephesians 4:27: "Neither give place to the devil." I need to stop giving the devil permission to run my life. But how do I do that? Just come to church every week? No, that won't do it. The devil is always looking for ways to make his home in us, but Paul is saying that we shouldn't leave any room for him to set up shop.

One thing we understand as believers is that Satan has been defeated. Jesus already took care of that. Satan may be defeated, but he hasn't been banished to the pit just yet. That's a little bit down the line, which means that he's still roaming around. Unfortunately for us, he likes to pick on believers more than anyone else. When Paul tells us that we shouldn't give any place to the devil, he's referring to everything else he mentioned before that. When you let your anger steer your decisions, you give Satan permission to come into you. Whenever you lose control, you give him permission to enter.

Has anyone ever told you that you have a bad attitude? You'd say, "What do you mean? I don't have a bad attitude. This is the way I always act." From the outside, they can see how unhealthy it is. But since we are all the sum total of our thoughts, sometimes we can't see beyond our own minds. It can be so hard to renovate and make these positive steps in the right direction.

When Paul is telling a church full of believers not to give any place to the devil, he's saying that we are not immune to the devil infiltrating our mindset either. Even though we walk and live in the name of the Holy Ghost, we have to be on guard for Satan, just like anyone else. As a matter of fact, we have to be even more aware than anyone else about what he is trying to do, because the devil has a preference for believers.

You can blame anything or anyone you want, but at the end of the day, it's all about how you think. What is your mindset towards yourself?

Look at today's environment. Everyone's crashing their cars into other people because they're in such a rush. The other members of the same body that are around us become obstacles rather than helping our brothers and sisters. Children are molested, people are mugged on the street, all because people are losing control of their own decision-making process. "If I want something, I deserve it. It doesn't matter how it makes anyone else feel or if it causes damage to the world around me. I want it, so I'll take it."

You must start feeding your mind some different material. We are at war when it comes to our minds. Everyone carries a cell phone with them, but we forget how powerful they actually are. We could start a war right now without having to leave the sofa. There are all sorts of filth on the internet, and we can fill our heads with it in a couple seconds flat. But it should be clear to us now that what we've been feeding our brains for all these years isn't doing us any good. It's time to start dieting.

I once worked at a gas station many, many years ago. I was changing tires, and I met this guy who was the mechanic there. Working with him, I picked up a few things and learned my way around a car. Vehicles were much simpler back then, though. There weren't nearly as many moving parts.

But over the years, cars have gotten more sophisticated. They have computers in them now that tell you when to buy gas, when to get an oil change, and when to fill up your tires with air. There's a Mercedes-Benz out there that drives itself. You don't even need to touch the steering wheel. I don't know about you, but I'm nowhere near ready for that. I want to control the car that I'm driving. I'm not prepared to sit in a car and let it rocket down the road at 80 miles per hour without my hands on the steering wheel. To me, that doesn't seem natural.

All technology has changed drastically over the years. When you pop the hood of a car now, all you see is a flat panel. You used to see a carburetor. Now, even the spark plugs are tucked away. For a guy like me that learned to work on cars back in the day, it's almost impossible to apply any of that knowledge to a car that just came out last year.

If I actually wanted to pursue being a mechanic today, I'd have some serious re-learning to do. I'd have to fill my head with all sorts of new information that would contradict what I learned before. As a matter of fact, there are colleges out there that offer automotive engineering classes. In the old days, it was so much easier. There wasn't really that much to work on. But now, it's all technology-based. When you take that thing in to get serviced, they just hook it up to a computer. I have a computer that tells me it's time to change this and time to change that, and when I see a mechanic, they just plug it into a different computer to see what's wrong with it. Two hundred dollars later, I can drive again.

I'd have to learn all sorts of things to be a mechanic, sure. But do you have any idea what those guys make? If you can get a license to work on a Mercedes-Benz, you can rake in over $100,000 a year without getting a single drop of grease on you. People don't know that. It really would pay to spend my time and energy learning all about those cars.

In the old days, when you saw someone roll out from underneath a car, they'd be covered from head to toe in grease. If you go into a shop now, look at the floor. It's clean as can be! Everybody has these nice, pressed uniforms with name tags. When the work gets too nitty-gritty, they send that work out for someone else to do. They'll say, "Oh, we don't actually build real engines here. We just swap them out." Why? "Because we don't want all that grease on our uniforms!"

It's not just mechanics, though. No matter what you want to do in life, you're going to have to refill your head with knowledge that isn't in there already. If you want to be a lawyer, the same thing applies. If you are planning on becoming a teacher, the same thing applies. It's the education and the knowledge that equip us to navigate new territory. If we desire to change, we have to be willing to un-learn the old information and replace it with current, updated information.

With a high school diploma, the best you are going to get is a restaurant gig or some kind of service job. You might make management if you stick around long enough. But in the long haul, the one who pushes himself to get that Bachelor's or Master's is eligible for a whole new category of career options. If you don't have the education, the other guy has a leg up on you. If you want to make it to the next level, you have to empty out the old knowledge and refill your mind with the new knowledge.

The enemy likes to focus on your failures. He'll highlight them and bring them to the forefront of your mind. He says things like, "You've failed too many times. How can you ever bounce back from this?" God doesn't keep track of these like we think He does, but the devil knows about every single time we slip up. He's just waiting to throw each instance back in our face.

Any time a person has too many incomplete things in their life, they feel rejection. They get depressed because when they look back, they realize that they never actually followed through with anything. Everyone wants to have at least one thing that they can stand back and admire, like,

"See? I finished that. It's all done." Many of us are so afraid of failure that we don't even turn in the assignment. We forget that trying and failing is better than not applying ourselves at all.

Anyone who has too many unfinished endeavors in their life has a mindset that tells them things like, "I can't do anything. There must be something wrong with me. I can't finish anything I start. Everything always just blows up in my face." Did you know that's the enemy's voice? Can't you see what he's trying to do? He wants to drive you even deeper into despair.

Completing anything is hard. And not only is returning to something you never finished difficult, but it's also embarrassing. Imagine going back to school to get your diploma after you dropped out. The enemy will bother you relentlessly if you go through life with too many unfinished things. He will try to use every single one of them to make a space for himself in your life. We just can't leave the door unlocked like that. That's one reason why people drop out of school. Class after class, they fail until they finally say, "What's the use? I can't pass a class to save my life, so I'm just going to leave."

Let's look at Ephesians 4:28: "Let him that stole steal no more: but rather let him labour, working with his hands the thing which is good, that he may have to give to him that needeth." If you're a thief, you need to stop stealing. Whatever the nature of your behavior has been up until this point, abandon it. Whatever you struggle with, you need to do the exact opposite of what you've always done. It's the only way that old mindset finally dies. You have to be intentional about denying the old mindset until it's powerless against you.

Instead of stealing, go get a job and earn some money so you can give to those who genuinely need it. Instead of becoming obsessed with a physical man or woman, go love Jesus instead. I do want to clarify one point, though: If you plan on quitting something—anything at all—you need to have something to replace it with, and that something needs to be something that is better for you. Otherwise, you'll slip back into your old ways.

You can't just quit eating apple pie out of the blue. If it were that easy, everyone would be nice and slim. Try some apple pie that has no sugar in it. If you've been eating that same recipe for your entire life, it's going to be practically impossible to stop without some sort of replacement.

Paul says that thieves should stop stealing, but he doesn't end the sentence there. He wants them to do something instead—work! Just in case you never hear it again, God actually does want everyone to work, especially if you are able-bodied.

Today, we have a technology base in our society. It takes 30 minutes for some big machine to drill a hole that in years past would usually take 10 guys a full week if they did it by hand. We can't stay stuck in an old-school mindset forever. We have to adapt and understand that the old mindset can only get us so far. If you really want to be a contender in the world today, you can't cling to information that you learned decades ago. I know it's hard to let go of that, but it's time to grow up.

If I'm going to be effective, I need to do some changing. I need to change how I think, and I need to change my perspective on listening. I also need to change my perspective on punctuality, practice, and commitment. If I don't change my mindset, it won't be long before the person in charge has to tell me, "I can't use you. I don't have time to deal with people who are stuck in their old ways."

Ephesians 4:29 is a heavy hitter. Check this out: "Let no corrupt communication proceed out of your mouth, but that which is good to the use of edifying, that it may minister grace unto the hearers." Think about how many people use curse words on a daily basis. Some people curse in every sentence, just because that's the way they've always talked, and that's the way their friends speak. But in reality, a lot of people curse because they don't have the right vocabulary as a result of not being able to read. We could pick up a book and educate ourselves, but we can't stand reading, so we don't bother. We don't want to do the work.

So many of us forget that what we speak has an effect on our environment and surroundings. Words frame your environment, your mind, your interactions with other people, and your opportunities. Even if you're just joking around, cussing for the sake of cussing, it counts as corrupt communication. I used to cuss all the time when I was in the military, but I realized I had to change my thought process about it. If you don't deal with it right now, you'll get to a point where literally every other word that comes out of your mouth will be a foul one. You won't even be able to help anyone with what you say, and it may be correct. Profanity will become how you communicate, which is part of who you are.

If I know my communication is not pleasing to God, I need to find a different way to say whatever I'm trying to say or say something different entirely. If a sentence really has to come out of your mouth, let it be something good, something useful.

The other day, I crossed paths with a man that has been practicing law for 47 years. He was a very distinguished gentleman, but he told me a surprisingly vulgar joke. I didn't laugh or anything, so I kind of just stood there quietly. When I saw him again, he said, "I didn't mean to say that in front of you. I heard you talking about church." I said, "What you said has nothing to do with me, really. But it has everything to do with you." Do you think I want him representing me in the courtroom? He might cuss the judge out, and then you know I'd be toast.

It doesn't matter what level you are in the professional world, in your social circle, or anywhere else. A corrupt mindset could be inside of anyone. It doesn't matter if you're poor or rich or in between. A corrupt mindset affects us on an individual level, one person at a time. Corrupt words come out of a corrupt mind. The only way to change is to feed the mind with something that isn't corrupt.

Not all corrupt communication involves curse words, though. If you pray like this, "I hope you hear me, God. I've been praying for years. If you can hear me, do something for me right now." That doubtful and confused mindset lacks faith, and you can't see God moving in your life because you don't believe He will.

If what you have to say does not encourage, edify, or

build someone up, don't say it at all. Even if you have to scold someone, there's a way to do it without tearing them down. This may sound impossible to you right now, but every word you speak should be filled with encouragement and grace.

When Jesus spoke with Judas before the betrayal, He never scolded him. He knew exactly what Judas was going to do, but He never singled him out in a crowd or humiliated him. How could anyone do that? If you know someone is out to get you, it would be so easy to call them out and embarrass them. How is it that Jesus was able to endure hanging out with this man for three full years, knowing the entire time that he was going to sell Him out for a bag of silver?

Jesus had a different mindset than we have. He didn't come to judge or condemn Judas; He came to set him free. Judas didn't take advantage of that opportunity to be set free because his mindset was corrupt. You may not know this, but you can follow God and still have just as corrupt of a mindset as Judas.

What should you do to develop a new mindset and put on the new man? Feed your mind with the Word of God. If you don't like the Bible, feed your mind with some good textbooks. Put a different concept in your brain than what you already have. Then, you can watch that concept manifest itself in your thought patterns, your speech, your behavior, and your life.

If you have a drinking problem, switch to soda. Every time you get thirsty, grab a Sprite. I guarantee you, in two weeks, you will be done with beer for good. Intentionally do the opposite of what you've always done. Feed your mind the things that challenge the corruption of the old man.

Remember, Romans 10:17 says, "So then faith cometh by hearing, and hearing by the word of God."

4

✠

HAVING A JESUS MINDSET
Philippians 2:1-2

I believe that most of us are not experiencing what God has for us because we are still operating with the same old mindset we had before we were saved. We suffered from a delusion. We thought that simply accepting Jesus as our personal Savior is where it starts and stops. Everything else should turn out just fine without any more work on our part.

Nobody ever really told me that I had to change my thinking. When you start a new job, when you get married, when you have kids, you're not going into those situations, thinking, *Man, I can't wait to change everything about the way I think!* Our least favorite part of external change is making the internal changes that are necessary to fully adapt. When Jesus told the first disciples, "Follow me and I will make you fishers of men," they probably didn't realize that they would have to learn how to do everything all over again. It's a lot like going back to grade school as an adult. It might feel silly, but the fact is that you have to start over from the very beginning.

When I accepted Jesus as my Savoir, it didn't come with a little warning that I would also have to change my thinking. Everyone I knew, throughout my whole life, said things like, "It will be alright. God knows your heart." People in church made it seem like everything that was going to happen in my life from that point forward was completely up to God, and my work was done. It seemed like I didn't even have to be involved anymore. All I had to do was show up and set myself on autopilot. God would sprinkle some of His power on me and change my mind, my behavior, and my speech.

When I got saved, I thought that I'd wake up the next morning with brand-new hands. But when I woke up, my hands looked the same as they did the day before. I walked and talked the same way too. No one ever told me that I had to make any changes to go along with my salvation. I thought it just happened.

When I was in the military, they put me through a six-week basic training program specifically designed to change my thinking. The military forced me to go through a mindset change, because if I hung onto my old civilian mindset, I never would have survived in there. The military focuses on training and conditioning your mind along with your body every step of the way.

No matter how many years I went to church, no one ever pointed at some scripture and said, "You'll never survive in here unless you change the way you think." We're navigating our way through salvation with the same compass we used before we got saved. We keep trying to give God what we think He wants, or what we want Him to have, but He's constantly refusing it. And just because God doesn't cry and whine about how He doesn't want what we offer Him, we think He's happy with it.

Scripture gives us very clear and vivid evidence that everyone who follows God must undergo a mindset change, but we breeze right past it. When we read the Old Testament stories, we don't realize the major changes the prophets had to undergo in order to obey God.

We're trying to lend money with a borrower's mindset. How are you ever going to loan anybody anything if you're always thinking about borrowing from somebody else? God is trying to do incredible things through His children, and if we don't step up to the plate and make these internal changes, we'll have no idea how to follow when He leads.

Let me give you an example. If I ask anyone how to cook collard greens, they're going to base their cooking style off of what they've seen their mama or grandmama do in the kitchen. "Well, I just boil them for a long time with some turkey. You know, maybe a smoked neck bone, a turkey breast, or a wing." But it's been nutritionally proven that you don't have to boil collard greens to death. As a matter of fact, the longer you boil them, the fewer nutrients remain.

And even though you know that nutrition fact, you still cook them the same way. You think, "What's the problem with that? I'm just doing what they did." Oh, okay. So basically, that means you boil all the vitamins out of the greens, and you don't even care. You could fry them up in five minutes, and they'd be ready to go, but you're over there thinking, "I can't eat my greens unless they're cooked like my mama used to cook them."

It's worse for folks who get married and don't want to

change their thinking. "I want to do the same things I did when I was single, even though I'm married now. I don't see how that's a problem." And then there's a problem, of course. But we'd rather invite those serious problems into our lives instead of tearing out all of our old traditions and habits to transform our minds.

All of those useless fables and superstitions have no place in your life if you're a Christ-follower. He doesn't need any of that primitive slavery thinking, and neither do you. The problem is those stories and rituals make up the core of who you are, and nobody wants to sacrifice their core. A mindset change deliberately attacks what we believe and who we are, and it's so, so hard to let go of those things. We're more attached to them than we will admit.

But even if we allow ourselves to work with God through one single situation with our spouse, we can edify our marriage a hundred times. Tremendous positive change can only come about when we finally lay down our arms and give up that attitude that says, "I don't want anyone telling me what to do." When we say that, we forget that the term "anyone" includes God. We might as well be saying, "Hey God, don't even talk to me. I don't want Your guidance." The tricky part is that, if we don't do what God says, we'll wind up doing what someone else says instead.

Back in the day, the Philippian church had all sorts of things going on. Paul wrote an encouraging letter to them because they were at odds with each other within the church. Imagine that! What a catastrophe. Nothing can get done when the church is standing against itself. Nobody wanted to work together.

Paul was trying to remind the Philippians of the importance of like-mindedness and the power that is available to folks who will sacrifice to become one with someone else. That's the biggest roadblock that prevents like-mindedness today. "I'm selfish, and I don't want to sacrifice. At my core, I want it to be about me, myself, and I. The church as a whole has no place on my agenda."

Following Christ is not a ministry of self. It has always been a ministry of others first and then self. "I'm not putting myself last for anything or anyone. Last time I put myself last, I regretted it. I'm not doing that anymore. I don't care who is preaching, either. Unless Jesus comes down and tells me Himself, I'm not doing it."

When families act like that, children become prey for the enemy. They're left unprotected because people are too selfish to sacrifice for them. The system will suck them up and punish them for their behavior when they don't know how else to act because they've been left to fend for themselves. I'm lucky, though. My mama was willing to sacrifice so that I could grow up correctly. Many mothers and fathers today could care less about their children and say, "It's all about me. It's all about what I want." When you don't take care of your children, that's what you're saying.

The Philippian church was at odds with itself. Paul knows how important like-mindedness is, so he's trying to relay that idea to the church through his letter. Before we can experience the abundance of what God has and is, we need to learn this same lesson. It helps to remember that Jesus is the only one that consistently and deliberately demonstrated to us how a change of mindset renders us effective in operation for the kingdom's benefit. If you ever get lost, or you don't know where to look to realign yourself, use Him as a template. If we could emulate His mindset, we'd all be golden.

In Philippians 2:1-2, Paul says,

If there be therefore any consolation in Christ, if any comfort of love, if any fellowship of the Spirit, if any bowels and mercies, Fulfill ye my joy, that ye be likeminded, having the same love, being of one accord, of one mind."

Before an alcoholic can experience sobriety, they have to stop drinking liquor. Before a drug addict can experience a clean lifestyle, they have to stop using drugs. Before a believer can experience the things that are mentioned in the above verse, they have to make some changes in the way they think. These shifts have to be deliberate if we are really serious about changing for the better. Otherwise, we can't genuinely experience any of the beautiful fruits of a relationship with God.

When Paul met Christ on the road to Damascus, he was so set in his ways. His whole mission was centered around destroying anyone who even thought about worshiping Jesus. But on his way to do even more damage, he had an encounter with the God of heaven. It knocked him off his horse, and it did something to him that had never been done before: it put him in a position where he was totally, utterly helpless.

And the first word he uttered when he regained his composure was, "Lord!" He's thinking, "Lord, what do you want me to do?" That one experience switched his whole mission from giving orders to taking them. The first thing a disciple must understand is that you aren't meant to go around barking orders at people. You should be asking God what He wants you to do. That "don't tell me what to do" mindset just won't work anymore if you want to be a disciple.

God told Paul, "Go to this place, and I will tell you what you're supposed to do." He was patient and obedient, probably for the first time in his life, because that encounter was unlike any other. Maybe God is asking us today, "Have you really met Me? Because anyone who ever truly met Me has changed into a different person." We find a way to explain it away, though. "Be patient with me. God isn't through with me yet. He's still working with me on that." Oh, so He can create the universe in seven days, but He can't change your speech in 40 years?

When Paul talks about consolation, he means encouragement. And when he mentions the comfort of love, he's talking about the way that God comforts us. It's not like He's coming to hold our hand and hug us, even though sometimes, that's exactly what we want. Instead, the Holy Spirit brings the Word of God. And if the Word of God can't bring you comfort, what amount of good could a hug do anyway? That's only superficial.

God is inside of you, wanting to guide and lead and direct you, but in order for you to develop true fellowship, your mind needs to change, not His. God isn't telling us that our spirit needs to change. When I got born again, my spirit was good to go. My brain is where my desires and passions and frustrations come from, not my spirit. My mind needed to get on board with my spirit so that I could have true fellowship with the Holy Spirit.

Have you ever met anybody that is experiencing this type of interaction with God? They are different people. We don't have too many examples, either. I wonder what it's like to see somebody who is deep in fellowship with the Holy Ghost. A lot of folks go to church every Sunday, but after they leave, they are talking trash about other people, cussing, and doing everything they did before they went to church.

I should be able to tell if any married man is in fellowship with the Holy Spirit by how he treats his wife. I should be able to see it from a mile away. We don't think anybody is watching, though, so we stay stuck in our old habits. We need to let our light shine! Let our demonstration of the principles of God be so evident in our life that anyone we meet can see our good works. That will direct them to draw near to God, and He'll draw near to them.

We've been doing what every other Christian we know has done since we were old enough to attend church: pretending. We do it because, well, we saw others doing it. Nobody taught us anything different, and nobody demonstrated anything different. We need to break that cycle.

The military sends everyone to basic training. I don't care if you're going to be a general or a private. You have to go to basic training. Why? The military's philosophy is, "Your thinking is crooked, and we need to fix that before we can start working with you." If you say, "I don't want to go to basic," then the military ain't for you. The rebellious ones get dishonorably discharged, which makes it difficult for them once they leave.

Kids these days go to school and act how everybody else does. They want to look like everybody else looks too. But then, they show up on Sunday and say, "I'm a disciple."

We know from our earlier studies that God will exalt us if we humble ourselves. Without fellowship with God, there's no way He would elevate us to a position of power and authority. Some of us are saying, "Oh, I thought it was automatic! I thought being elevated to power just happened once I accepted Jesus." It doesn't work that way, though. We have to hold up our end of the bargain, which means maintaining fellowship. Before I can be raised to a position of power, I must have fellowship with the one who empowers me. I can't receive or dispense mercy without that fellowship, much less achieve greatness by the hand of God.

We are nothing but extensions of our parents, whether we want to admit it or not. A lot of us are just repeating what we saw play out in our own home. It's nothing new; it's been this way for ages. Breaking out of that pattern is going to challenge everything in me, and it's going to really disrupt who I am and the way I've been living. When Paul is talking to the church, he's not pulling instructions out of thin air. He's telling them exactly what he went through. If he wasn't made new, how on earth could he write letters of encouragement from prison?

They imprisoned Paul's hands and feet, but they couldn't touch his brain. He turned that over to Jesus long before he got locked up. We don't like to acknowledge this, but we all have areas in our life that we're not willing to surrender. We're still putting God in the backseat. Paul switched spots with God, which allowed him to stay in fellowship with Him through serious trials.

In Philippians 2:2, Paul says, "Fulfill ye my joy." Before you can experience any of the things in the first verse, you have to maintain that fellowship and carry out the things that make God smile.

When I was growing up, my mom used to work from 4 PM until midnight. She'd give us a list of chores before she left, and it was up to us to finish them all by the time she returned home. One of the tasks on the list was scrubbing the floor, and it was hard back then. Bleach and water, down on all fours—it wasn't pretty.

If the floor was dry by the time she returned home from work, she'd go to bed happy because she knew we did all the work early. But one night, I accidentally fell asleep before I did my part. I woke up around 10:30 in a panic because I realized I hadn't scrubbed the floor. After I calmed down a bit, I thought, *If I scrub it and dry up as much water as I can with the mop, and then put newspaper down, the newspaper will soak up the excess water. I could just throw the newspaper away right before she gets home.*

But I didn't know that I was going to fall asleep again. She walked in the door, and all she saw was newspaper all over the floor, which meant I didn't do what she said when she said to do it. I did it at another time, which means I didn't follow her directions exactly. People don't like to do what they are told, even though the Bible clearly states that obedience is better than sacrifice. She didn't come into the house shouting at the top of her lungs, but let's just say that it only took one slip-up like that to set a brother straight. We should be that quick to change our mindset when we fall short of our duties as the children of God.

What would it look like if we fulfilled God's joy? Jesus had a mindset that was always in perfect sync with the Holy Ghost. Can you imagine that? We don't even believe that's possible. Like-mindedness means being willing to give up something so that you and your brothers can get along. Getting along with my brothers and sisters is more important than having my own way. If I have my way, that's all I have. If we get along, we all get what we want.

That's what families used to do. In modern times, there is no actual concept of family in the house. The problem is that we wind up picking and choosing who our brothers and sisters should be. We love only those we have fellowship with, and even in the church, we withhold that fellowship so we can maintain control of our social surroundings. We clique up with those who think alike, and we all kind of believe in the same thing, so we don't let anyone else in. That's why, when people visit a church for the first time, they don't feel included. They can sense that separatism.

They see you over there with your crew every Sunday. When they try to interact with you, you say, "No, thanks. We sort of have our own thing going on." When was the last time you invited a stranger to lunch after church? We all know that birds of a feather flock together, but they also gossip and cause all kinds of trouble. That's why God warns us against cliquing up like that. Whether you're in the church or outside of it, segregating yourself like that is only going to divide the body further. And since we're trying to achieve one mind, we can't keep drawing lines and excluding people.

We've been talking about being of one accord and having one love and not the emotional, romantic love that plays favorites, either. This kind of love levels the playing field. I should be able to love two different people exactly the same. This doesn't mean that you have one template of love that you apply to everyone because you don't need what your brother or sister needs. Everyone is different. Instead, it means always turning to the Spirit of God to find out the best way to love everyone you meet. We need to do what's best for every single person we come across as instructed by the Holy Ghost, no matter what that means we might have to give up.

In essence, we are trying to love like God loves. He does for us what's best, and He gives us what we actually need, not what we want. Even though we think we do, we don't truly know what we want.

Have you ever tried to please someone based on what they say? Have you ever dated someone who doesn't know what they want? You're so busy trying to get a handle on what they tell you they want that you forget to be yourself, and the relationship crumbles. But when I align my mind with the Holy Ghost, He'll tell me what you need, and I'll love you that way. I could spend my whole life trying to figure out how to make you happy, or I can just let God satisfy and fulfill you.

When you hear about Jesus coming back for a church without spot or blemish, I doubt He means that He's going to be keeping tabs on who's wearing the right clothes. I believe He's saying that He wants to see a church with the right mindset. That's great because the people with that mindset will already be seeking God anyway. And if all of this like-mindedness talk seems obvious, and it makes perfect sense to us, why don't we do it? Why am I so selfish? Why would I rather have my own way than budge a single inch for the good of someone else?

Babies are selfish and cry when there is nothing wrong. Babies want what everybody else has, and they're never satisfied with what they have. Grown folks are supposed to be able to act mature. However, so many of us are still acting like infants when it comes to our inability to see beyond ourselves. The truth is that we need help, and not just every once in a while; we need all the help we can get, whenever we can get it.

I have to lean on the Holy Ghost all the time. I wake up in the morning, praying for that like-mindedness. I have a desire to grow in that direction, but it's not that easy. I need some serious help. My selfishness gene will kick in unexpectedly, and then my ignorance gene will run off and say something stupid. To be completely frank, I need help controlling my own natural stupidity. And if I didn't cling to God for help, I'd be in jail before sundown. My thinking gets warped sometimes, and if that's all I have, there's no chance I'm going to make it.

In Acts 2, what does it look like when folks are in one accord? Yes, this passage is very popular, but I want to show you what is possible when everyone has the same mindset. Jesus told John to wait for the promise, which was the Holy Ghost. It had been 50 days since His resurrection (actually, that's how the term "Pentecost" came about, from the Greek for 50th day). When the day of Pentecost arrived, they were all in one place, in one accord.

Now, there were men and women present there. Imagine that! The Holy Ghost can work in males and females. It's not about gender; it's always been about mindset. We keep saying, "I'm a woman, I think differently than a man," and vice versa. Did you know that you aren't supposed to be a woman? You're actually supposed to be a disciple, and you're one that just happens to be a woman. That makes you think like a disciple, not a woman.

Men and women can't see eye to eye when they have different mindsets. I will never see eye to eye with you if I keep saying, "I'm a man, and God made me this way." Did He now? Did He make me that way? Or am I just holding onto that way because it's easier than changing? The last time I checked, He said that anyone who walks by the Spirit is a son of God—not a man or woman of God, but a son of God. The Spirit is supposed to be the basis for our mindset. We just happen to be male or female.

And when the day of Pentecost was fully come, they were all with one accord in one place. And suddenly, there came a sound from heaven as of a rushing mighty wind, and it filled all the house where they were sitting (Acts 2:1-2).

They weren't all scattered around Jerusalem in chaos,

doing whatever they wanted. Everyone was with one another, in one place, waiting for the promise, just as Jesus instructed. And wherever there's like-mindedness, the spirit of God has freedom of operation. He isn't confined to one or two people; He can use everything and everyone in an atmosphere like that.

Check out Acts 2:44-45. This happened after the day of Pentecost, and after Peter preached the first sermon to 5,000 people. After he preached the second sermon, 3,000 joined with them.

And all that believed were together, and had all things in common; And sold their possessions and goods, and parted them to all men, as every man had need.

They said, "Whatever I have isn't mine anymore; it's ours." As long as you keep guarding your stuff as yours and not the kingdom's, we are going to have issues. If God doesn't have access to what you own, how can you expect Him to use it? His will is going to get done one way or another, but you probably won't be included in the process.

Some of us wouldn't be so quick to get rid of everything like that, right? We'd say, "I need confirmation before I do that. I need to go into prayer and make sure that's actually what He said." So God says there's a need, but you have reservations? Someone needs to get their mind right. Once that happens, God can use you for all sorts of amazing things.

There's a church near me here in Florida that was built on the faith of six people. Not 600. Not 6,000. Just six. It doesn't take an army. God doesn't need everybody. He just needs those who are like-minded, and He will make it happen. It's just a matter of whether or not you want to be included in God's program. Six people built a facility that cost over $600,000, and none of them are even at that church anymore. God is using them for other things, but for a while, that was what they were supposed to do.

You can't worry about who is going to take part in what. If it's a kingdom thing, I'm going to do it. Some of us are so particular. "I ain't doing nothing unless I get to sit where I want to sit. I ain't giving nothing up unless my family gets a pew all to themselves." When was the last time your entire family has been to church at one time? And now you want your own pew because you donated $25? That's not kingdom work, and that's not generosity. You just want to be known as a person who donated.

We know that oneness is something that God asks from His children, but can it work in the lives of those who are not believers? Of course. That's why the world can do more than the church can sometimes. They come together and feed thousands, and we can't even feed ourselves.

The world can accomplish more than we can because they are willing to set aside their differences for a cause, while we're here with our issues, refusing to come together. We need to be one with the Lord! A number of entertainers will come together and write a song to feed people. Folks from all walks of life will band together for one common cause and raise enough money to feed a whole country, but many people of God (who say they have the power of God behind them) won't put aside their differences for the kingdom's agenda.

Let's look at Genesis 11:1-6, where we hear the story of the Tower of Babel.

And the whole world was of one language, and of one speech. And it came to pass, as they journeyed from the east, that they found a plain in the land of Shinar, and they dwelt there. And they said one to another, Go to, let us make brick, and burn them thoroughly And they had brick for stone, and slime had they for mortar. And they said, Go to, let us build us a city and a tower, whose top may reach unto heaven; and let us make us a name, lest we be scattered abroad upon the face of the whole earth. And the Lord came down to see the city and the tower, which the children of men builded. And the Lord said, Behold, the people is one, and they have all one language; and this they begin to do: and now nothing will be restrained from them, which they have imagined to do.

All of these people have one thing in mind: building a tower. But a project like that needs so many different things in order to work. Some people had to transport the brick; others had to get the mud to make the bricks. Some had to operate the kettle to burn the bricks, while still others had to lay the bricks.

It's difficult to get Christians to work together like this, though. Most people want to do the highest-level job. However, it takes all kinds of gifts to run the kingdom, and they all originate from the same place—the Holy Ghost. We always tend to want the one that looks the most important. "I don't only want to be heard; I have to be seen. I'm not going to get the brick, because nobody is going to see that. I want them to see me make the brick and acknowledge my craftsmanship."

But these people working on the tower had no problem splitting up to get the job done. Could you imagine being one of the people that had to get the slime? The slime was just mud so that was a messy job. You don't hear anyone arguing, though. Everyone just does their part.

Did you notice how almost every verse says, "Let us"? They're trying to build a tower that would reach into heaven, but for themselves alone. They weren't trying to reach God. They didn't know anything about God. They were just a group of people who set a goal and became like-minded in order to achieve it.

They knew that if they didn't come together and erect a city, other nations would come in and scatter them to the four winds. They wanted to establish something and make a name for themselves. There was no God in the picture, and it was going just fine until the Holy Ghost looked down at them.

When God takes a second to examine the people, His first thought is, *Wow! These people are one. They have one language, and they have one idea. With this kind of mindset, nothing will be impossible for them.*

But in the very next verse, the whole story shifts. "Go to, let us go down, and there confound their language, that they may not understand one another's speech." The problem with their plan is pretty obvious, right? They left God out. Their labor had no kingdom agenda attached. I find it interesting that God didn't interrupt the building process. Instead, He just interrupted the communication process.

When He gave all of them a different language, it tore them apart. God knew that people who are of one mind are powerful. If He didn't do something to intervene, nothing would ever stop a people that united.

Many years later, Paul would suggest that this happened because like-mindedness was reserved for the church. Since the church hadn't been established yet, and nothing on earth was going to happen without God instituting it, He had to step in. The victory, which can only be achieved through like-mindedness, was being saved for us.

Paul is warning the church, "Don't let your one accord be destroyed by selfishness or petty jealousies. The kingdom is bigger than just you. It's bigger than two of you, bigger than five of you. If you can just work together for a kingdom agenda, I guarantee you, all your needs will be met. If you can do that, you'll never go without being satisfied."

You might believe that thinking alike will make you blend in, and you'll eventually be overlooked. However, the kingdom doesn't operate like that. It functions best when everyone sacrifices for the same thing, and then God rewards each of them according to their needs.

5

HAVING A JESUS MINDSET, PART II

Philippians 2:3-4

Throughout this book, we're discovering that both God and the enemy want to infiltrate our minds. That's where the battle is fought. We all struggle to keep our mind focused on the things of God. We have a real desire to maintain that focus, but day by day, we're finding out just how hard that can be.

It's not as though people can say, "Just focus on God!" To be honest, I can't even focus on TV for too long. My mind will wander a little, and before I know it, all sorts of things come in to occupy that space. Our circumstances can distract us, especially when they get serious, but it's our responsibility as believers to keep our focus zeroed in on God. In order to experience the things that are associated with our relationship with God, we absolutely have to.

Many people never truly change when they get to church. I guess they genuinely come to the Lord, but you never see their lives move in a different direction. They still talk the same way, act the same way, and think the same way, because no one tells them that a mindset change is required in order to follow Christ.

Jesus told the first disciples, "Follow Me. You have to leave where you are. You have to leave your way of thinking and acting if you really want to follow Me." Most of us were never taught that in church. We learned about the cross, and we celebrate the cross, but sometimes we don't truly understand what we're celebrating.

When something has had a hold of your mind for a lifetime, it does not want to let go. I don't care how much you dress it up. I believe that we have to preach and teach in line with what is happening today, so people will know that change is absolutely necessary.

When you go off to college, you need to undergo a mindset change. If you think your mama is going to be calling in every morning just to wake you up, you are going to flunk in no time. For every transition in life, adaptation is key. If you don't make the appropriate changes to the way you think and live, you'll fall flat on your face.

Some of you want promotions, but you don't want responsibilities. There's no such thing as a bigger, better job without more on your plate! You're not going to land a $100,000-a-year job with zero responsibilities attached. When you make that much money, you're supposed to take calls after office hours. You're supposed to wake up at the crack of dawn on Sunday and get to work, while everybody else is enjoying their day off. If they're paying you a hundred grand, you better answer that phone every time it rings, no matter what.

It's the same with Christ. I'm sure you remember Romans 12:2. "And be not conformed to this world: but be

ye transformed by the renewing of your mind, that ye may prove what is that good, and acceptable, and perfect will of God." The rebellious mind does not want to be brought under the rule of anything. Unfortunately, the rebellious mind is ultimately fearful of being ruled, and what you think is setting you free could actually be enslaving you.

You know, Apple is a cutting-edge company. Whenever they want you to buy a new device, they just make a newer iphone operating system (iOS). When you download that to your device, which used to work just fine, it starts to act wonky. When you call and tell them what's going on, they say, "Oh, that's because of the new iOS. Maybe you should get a newer phone so it can keep up with the operating system. That 6+ was good last year, when you got it, but now we need you to get the 7." Even though they tell you that it only does three things differently than the phone you have now, you still feel like you need it in order to keep up.

Did you notice that the first and second generation iPad doesn't even exist anymore? When the iPad Pro first came out, I thought, "It's way too big" at 12.7 inches tall, 9.6 inches wide. But it is lighter than the iPad 2 and even lighter than the Air 2. When you hold the Air 2 up against it, it looks like a giant, but when you use it, you can hold the iPad pro with two fingers. The new one has amazing graphics, and I can use a pencil on it! It does everything I need it to do, but I didn't want to hear about it at first. All I had to do was shift my focus from the old to the new, and Apple's marketing strategy took care of the rest. Let's look at Philippians 2:3-4. Christ's joy is that we be like-mindedness.

Let nothing be done through strife or vainglory; but in loneliness of mind let each esteem other better than themselves. Look not every man on his own things, but every man also on the things of others.

Why does Paul tell the church of Philippi not to do anything through strife or vainglory? What makes that so important? You should remember that the church was at odds with itself. Brothers and sisters were sitting on different sides of the fence. In many passages of scripture, strife can mean anger, but in this verse, it has more to do with self-interest.

Corinthians tells us that we should do every single thing to the glory of God. I know that if I do anything through my own self-interest, motivated by how something would benefit me, I'd be doing it for the wrong reason.

Imagine a vocalist that says, "I can't sing backup; I'm a soloist." Why? Because you want people to see you. Scripture tells me that everything I do, everything I eat, and everything I drink should be for the glory of God, right? There's no room in there for me, my glory, or my self-interest.

I was always taught to make sure that me, myself, and I get taken care of. But now, I have to shift gears and realize that more than 99% of the time, what I do to glorify God is going to be done for somebody other than me.

Now, I have to change how I relate to other folks— people who are like me and people who aren't. You may not always be able to see what my mindset is towards you, but God knows. There's no sense in trying to elevate yourself when you aren't willing to elevate God or anyone else. You've got it all backwards.

If you want a Jesus mindset, you have to be all about glorifying God and be satisfied in that. If I lift you up, He will lift me up. But He isn't going to lift me up until it's my season to be lifted up. Most of us can't handle God because He waits so long to elevate us that we get impatient and jump ship.

People in the church are busy watching everybody else to determine what their motivation is when we ought to keep an eye on ourselves instead. I need to make sure that whatever I'm doing at any given moment is for His glory. That term, "vainglory," has to do with the desire to be praised.

That's what Judas' problem was. He was always following Christ for his own selfish interest, never looking to elevate Him. Jesus knew that and didn't stop him from tagging along. That's why no one will prevent you from coming to church.

Paul is saying that if you want God to notice you and you want to pursue a relationship with Him, He has to be your motivation. Even when we pray, the first order of business is to glorify Him. Everything else is secondary. We shouldn't want to do anything for empty praise.

Some of us were raised in tough environments where we've never been properly acknowledged for any accomplishments. It's hard for us to remember a single time when people we respected gave us accolades for anything. And since we didn't receive any, sometimes we come to God wanting to be praised, simply because we have never experienced accolades for ourselves.

Glorifying God has to do with how you treat the people around you. God doesn't need your seat on the bus or for you to buy Him some food. God doesn't need you to visit Him in jail. No jail could hold Him, anyway. But Jesus gives us a crazy idea: "When you do this to the least of these, my brethren, you do it for Me." The church should be visible in the community, continually doing things for others. That's the only way some people get to see the love of God. If we're meeting indoors every Sunday to say that God is good without going out into the streets on Monday to demonstrate that, what did Sunday mean to us?

Take a look at Galatians 5:26. When Paul writes to the church, he says, "Let us not be desirous of vain glory, provoking one another, envying one another." That kind of mindset provokes jealousy among the believers. When you see someone getting credit for something, and their motive is wrong, don't you wish that it was you receiving it instead? Watching that happen enough times might make a believer abandon his morals just to adopt the other way of doing things. After all, it worked, right? They got rewarded, didn't they? But we need to remember this one thing: envy is not a characteristic of the Holy Ghost.

None of us should desire self-motivated praise above all else. For example, imagine that I was the kind of pastor who said, "You know what? I just want them to scream every time I preach." That means I'd have to say everything you like, how you like it, and when you like it, which would cause me to withhold some of God's truth from you, and you'd leave church without being fed. I had to ultimately realize that God's desire for you to grow is greater than my desire for applause.

There's something in all of us that doesn't like to be booed. "Uh-oh, here she comes… She's always talking about that God stuff. Give me a break." Nobody wants to be treated like that. The only way you are going to be able to stand against that attitude is if you undergo a mind transformation. When people react that way to us, we have to approach them with confidence. "I know how they're going to act. I know what they're going to say, but it's not going to stop me from approaching them."

Jesus knew what would eventually happen to Him as He was riding into Jerusalem. He didn't respond the way either side wanted Him to, though. He had His own agenda that was given to Him by God, and He didn't care who it upset. When He showed up, everyone was praising Him and throwing palm leaves down at His feet. Two weeks later, those same people were shouting, "I don't care what you do, just kill him and get it over with!"

The Word of God is there to overhaul our thinking, and I need that. Changing our thinking isn't an overnight process. Remember when you learned how to swim? It takes more than one lesson. It doesn't stop there, either. Swimming in shallow water is different than swimming in deeper water. In shallow water, you think, "I can stand up whenever I need to." But when you hit 12 feet, try to stand up and watch what happens. You need confidence to navigate the deeper water, and that takes repetition and practice. That's why pools are designed in four-foot increments.

You stretch your abilities gradually. In the same way, the Word of God is there to retool our thinking and help us develop in increments through stages of faith.

We all have to undergo that. It's not just you or me. When I get to heaven, I won't have to learn how to praise. It will be automatic. But here on earth, we have to learn how. We battle against our old nature to take these steps in the right direction.

It's amazing how quickly we say that we don't like things we've never tried. We've heard other folks say something isn't good, so we just go with that, not bothering to try it for ourselves. But how are we supposed to know that the person who told us that something wasn't good ever tried it themselves? They could have just heard it from someone else too.

I'll be the first to admit it. I still struggle with the things my mama and grandmama told me. "Put a horseshoe over your door to keep the evil spirits out." Every front door you walked in had a horseshoe over it. The same people who proclaim the benefits of the horseshoe march into church every Sunday, saying, "Jesus is the way, the truth and the life..." But they need the horseshoe too.

They didn't know any better, though. Their parents told them, and they told us. We did it out of not knowing. But then God said, "You are not ignorant anymore. Let me re-train your thinking." You'll know that your thinking has truly changed when you can take that horseshoe down without being afraid of evil spirits coming in. Sure, you love Jesus and everything, but that's not the issue. We need to break free from a mindset that we've been indoctrinated with since we came out of the womb.

Even home remedies can have a little superstition tied in. Back in the day, if you stepped on a nail, you would put a penny and some fatty meat on it. Back then, we went barefoot all the time, so this was pretty common. We'd just press the copper and the fatty meat on the wound together, and that would draw out the poison.

You can't do that anymore. First of all, the modern penny is not made out of copper. And nowadays, health standards require that you get a tetanus shot, so don't even bother using that remedy. Just get a tetanus shot and move on with your life. Things aren't like they used to be. These ideas were given to us by people we respected and trusted. It's so hard to drop them all of a sudden after a lifetime of hearing and repeating these old fables.

Now, back to scripture. From verse 4, we know that the mindset of Jesus does not conform to this world. The person that's operating in the mindset of the Holy Spirit does not do anything for self-gratification or credit. Instead, it's all for God's glory.

Paul keeps describing this mindset, warning the church against only caring for their own things. Selfishness is a giant issue in the church today, and most of this selfishness is birthed out of disobedience.

This is not to say that everybody in the church is going to be mature automatically. There will always be stages of growth in the body of Christ. Still you would hope that everyone who spends some time within these walls would experience some sort of attitude adjustment after a while.

The main idea is that selfishness is not something that glorifies God. Keep in mind that Jesus didn't come to earth for Himself, and He didn't come for you, either. He came because that's what God wanted Him to do. Even though His mission benefited us, it was ultimately for God.

I know how that sounds, and we want to argue that point. But if we did, Jesus would say, "No, I came because my Father sent me. I came to do His will. It just so happens that you are going to benefit from it." The motivation never came from you—it came from God. Come for the right reason, do it for the right reason, and God will make sure You get resurrected on the third day. Does that make sense?

But, again, we've been conditioned to look out for ourselves. We see it everywhere. We're afraid that if we elevate someone else, we'll get put down. That's the way the world works. If I acknowledge you, if I edify you, if I esteem you, I will get put down. That's just the way we have been taught to understand in the world.

God says, "It's a different day. I have to change your thinking about that. When you esteem someone other than yourself, the person you esteem is going to be elevated. Guess what I'm going to do for you? If my Word is true, you reap what you sow. If you sow esteem into somebody else, I have to esteem you. You can't give something away with a genuine mindset that I can't give you back. If I couldn't do that, then my Word would be a lie. And before my Word lies, heaven and earth would pass away."

The world has us so afraid of changing. We think, "If I

look out for anyone but myself, if I don't do it for myself, then I will get run over." But God says, "I want to change your thinking. Be quiet and humble. Sit back and watch how much I celebrate you."

It's important to clarify that, when we talk about looking out for each other, we don't mean that you should ignore your situation. Some of us have problems that can't be ignored. There's nothing wrong with taking care of business, but we all need to remember to serve in order to keep selfishness and fear from creeping in and calling the shots.

I hope you know that maturing in Christ has no numbers attached to it. It's all about the maturing of the mind and the spirit, and that doesn't necessarily correspond with particular ages of the physical body.

That means we can train a baby. Yes, babies can barely talk, but if we just start working with them and teaching them certain principles, when they become old enough to walk and talk, they will walk and talk like Jesus. Our mindset is this: "They are too young to know that. They are just kids. They need to play right now." Don't you know that kids are more resilient than adults? They can play and learn at the same time. We're the ones with the rigid mind. I can only do one thing at a time, and on some days, barely so.

Have you ever given a child a cell phone? What did they do with it? You can hand a baby a cell phone, and that baby, through their own intellect, will eventually learn how to work that thing better than I can. Who are we to say that they are not ready to learn about what God said?

But we keep holding back. "They're just too young. They are not too young to get indoctrinated by technology, but they are too young to get indoctrinated by the Word of God." We make a conscious decision not to prepare them because we think they can't handle it when God is showing us very clearly that they can. So, what do we do? We wait until we think they're old enough. But by then, they are so rebellious that they won't learn.

We simply don't believe in our children. We say, "Don't make my baby sit down. She's just too young. Babies can't sit still." But they can sit still if they learn in increments. If I can get them to sit still for one minute at a time, eventually they will turn that into an hour. It's hard to get grown folks to sit still. Most of us sit still now because we don't have the strength to move. It takes too much effort. Now, if we were 25 and those knees worked like they used to, we'd be all over the place. But since we can't, we claim that others aren't ready either.

When I was growing up, you couldn't take a break after you had a baby, not while you were raising six other children, cooking meals, washing clothes, and everything else. My mom had to teach us how the system works from day one. Once she had fed you, bathed you, dried you, and laid you on the bed with that plastic underneath you so you wouldn't wet the bed, and you'd cry for no reason, she just wouldn't come. She was trying to teach us that there's no sense in crying when nothing is wrong.

It's all about your maturity. We learned very early. When a baby was crying, there was one of two things wrong, the baby was wet or hungry. Change them, feed them, and lay them back down on their plastic. When you got fed, bathed, dried, and laid down, it meant that it was time to shut up and go to sleep!

If you train them from day one, they start learning at a very young age. But when you let your baby sleep on your chest every single night, you train them to think that is the only way they can fall asleep. That's lovely and everything, but there's just one problem with that—when are you going to sleep?

I've noticed that we are very good at trying to change other folks to be like God, but we don't want to change and be like God ourselves. Let's read Romans 15:1-3.

We then that are strong ought to bear the infirmities of the weak, and not to please ourselves. Let every one of us please his neighbor for his good to edification. For even Christ pleased not himself; but, as it is written, The reproaches of them that reproached thee fell on me.

This passage gives us a little context that helps us understand what he's talking about in Philippians. I have witnessed this all my life in church. Folks that have been in church for a long time have no tolerance for those that are just coming in. They have an expectation (I don't know where they get it from) that the person who just wandered in off the street should act exactly like them. But if I looked closely enough at some of those church people, they'd wind up setting a pretty poor example.

Let's take a second to examine how some of them act. They don't give. They're always gossiping. You find them in the midst of all kinds of negativity. They're never regular attendees at church, Bible study, or anything else. Any time you come across any confusion or drama, they are right there at the center of it. This is what church folk expect of new believers.

First of all, newcomers should dress a certain way when they show up. "If you're coming to my church, you need to look a certain way." People always ask me, "Do I have to wear a suit?" I say, "Not if you don't have one. If you do have one, and you want to wear it, that's your choice. I'm not interested in clothes at all. It's your soul that should be important. Your soul is naked, so there's no sense in trying to clothe that with the right outfit you wear."

Anyway, let's get back to the text. He says, "we that are strong," and strength has to do with mental maturity in this verse. Now, none of us will ever evolve to the level of Christ's mindset because He was highly developed in his faith. To us, it's a continual and repeated process on a day-by-day basis. We are constantly growing, maturing, and improving in our faith. That's why "glory to glory" and "faith to faith" are mentioned so often. That means our mindset is evolving into the mindset of Christ more and more with each passing day. When we finally reach maturity, we will be out of here.

Those of us who have matured in the word of God should have strength to be able to bear the weakness in faith of those who have just come in. We should not expect the same maturity of a person who just became a part of God's family on Sunday that we require of someone who has been here for years. To think that way is very immature. They haven't had the exposure. They need training and discipling before I can require anything of them.

The entire church should never become about anyone at all besides Jesus. Those who think they're strong don't know the meaning of the word. Strength isn't just attending church regularly. Being strong means that I as a pastor can use you for the kingdom's agenda. We can't raise up a church where folks are trying to instruct people in what they themselves are not living by. That's hypocritical. We who are strong ought to bear the infirmities of the weak and not simply please ourselves.

Is there anywhere in the scripture where Christ looked out for somebody who was weak? Yes, sir. Judas was weak, wasn't he? They all were weak, but Jesus bore their weakness in faith. He was tolerant, patient, loving, and kind with them. And when they needed a particular scolding, He did so in love.

What would it look like if the Savior of the world was blunt with them, like, "You've been with me for 30 days now. You ought to be able to handle this whole cross thing." He didn't do that to them, though, and we know that. When the scripture talks about the mindset of Christ, that mindset has to be one with the patience to deal with a person who has not developed in their faith to the level that you have. How you respond to that person says a lot about what kind of mindset you've developed.

Verse 2 says, "Let every one of us please his neighbor for his good to edification." Again, that's unselfish behavior. The term "please" has to do with serving one another. That's the beauty of a mature mindset. A mature believer can serve anyone—even an enemy. God isn't necessarily asking you to hug them, but you can't do what God wants you to do for them unless you've developed a level of mental maturity that rises above your selfish urge to leave them out.

And now for the kicker in verse 3: "For even Christ pleased not himself." Then what's my excuse? Christ didn't come to earth to serve Himself. Christ didn't come to die for His salvation. He didn't come to renew a relationship between Himself and God. He and God were doing just fine, but we were torn up and needed God.

Because of His mature mindset, He was able to deal with our weaknesses, and therefore, all of the sins that we have committed. God told Jesus to take all of that on, but only because He had a mature mindset. He was strong enough to deal with it. "Jesus, You do without, because they can't. You take this on because they can't. You deal with all of this, because they can't. You are not only the oldest child, but You are the example."

When I was growing up, that's what they used to tell the oldest child. "You are the oldest, so you need to set an example for your brothers and sisters." It was a requirement in my house that the oldest sibling set the standard for the younger ones to follow. In this case, Jesus set the standard. Everything God disapproved of, everything that disappointed God wasn't dumped on us. He had to send someone with a different mindset to take it on, and that Someone was innocent of it all. That's what the strong bearing the infirmities of the weak looks like. Those of us who have been doing this ought to be able to walk with those who are weaker and protect them. God is not asking us to do anything that Jesus hasn't already done.

You have a desire for everyone to like you—I mean, really like you. Well, I'm here to tell you that you are in the wrong game. See if you can partner more with folks who don't like you, especially when you are traveling down Discipleship Boulevard and not Church Member Boulevard. When you are headed towards being like-minded and operating like Jesus, you will come across plenty of folks who won't approve of that.

Jesus was killed by the ones who were supposed to have a similar mindset. I wish I could tell you that wanting to be liked will serve you well when working for God, but I know that it won't. It won't serve you well at work, at school, or anywhere else. There's so much more to it than that.

6

HAVING A JESUS MINDSET, PART III

Philippians 2:7-9

As we search through the scriptures, we are discovering
that we operate under different mindsets in every stage of
our life. Different mindsets are not just something that affects our relationship with God. We are slowly learning
that nearly any form of failure is the result of an incorrect
mindset. Why are we so resistant? We don't like change, of
course. No one does. When you talk about change, especially if it requires us to live differently, we don't want to
hear it. It's just a part of our human nature. We want
things to stay exactly the way they've always been so that
we never have to adapt or adjust.

The truth is we all love to be in control. The second
someone compromises that, we just want to shut our ears
and look the other way. This hunger for power, like most of
our other characteristics, is a result of how we were raised.
Whether you as a parent talk to your child every day or
never at all, you are imparting a mindset on them and impacting the way they will grow and live their lives.

I wonder how many of us think that a Jesus mindset ap-
pears in no time flat, like God just flips a coin and everything changes. Even Jesus had to undergo a serious

transformation of the mind. And if you don't think He did, just remember that none of us have ever left a position of deity to become human.

You can claim that you've made giant shifts all you want by saying, "Well, I had to learn to love white people. I had to learn to love police officers. That was hard for me." But let's be honest. Nothing trumps Jesus coming here to serve instead of staying up there with the Holy Spirit and angels worshiping Him. Nothing you will ever change can impress me when Jesus made the transition from Creator to creature.

I know you've given up all sorts of things. I know you've sacrificed a lot. I know you don't do the things you used to do, and that was a difficult process for you. But Jesus went from speaking light into existence to having to manually light a candle. Don't let yourself get all high and mighty because you've made a few shifts here and there in your personal life. No matter what you changed, what you sacrificed, or what you gave up, Jesus gave more. Let's keep that in mind as we dig into the scripture for a bit.

In Philippians 2:5-9, Paul is talking to the church in Philippi, and it's interesting that he's always bringing up this idea of mindset when speaking to the children of God. He specifically talks about it in the letters he wrote to the church, without really mentioning it to anyone outside of the body of believers.

In Corinthians, Philippians, and Colossians, he's always writing to churches and giving personal testimonies about the dramatic change that he underwent when he met Jesus on the road to Damascus. His life was completely turned around, so he just kept telling his story to himself

Sometimes we forget that Paul was not among the original twelve. He calls himself an apostle born out of due time. He received his instructions from Jesus by way of the Holy Ghost Himself. This information he shares with the church is from a one-on-one lesson he had with Jesus that gave him priceless insight into what Christ had to undergo in order to descend to the earth and do what He did for us.

When God asks you to sacrifice, it shouldn't feel like a big deal to you if your mindset is right. As a matter of fact, it should feel like a welcome turn of events.

Philippians 2:5-9 says,

Let this mind be in you, which was also in Christ Jesus: Who, being in the form of God, thought it not robbery to be equal with God: But made himself of no reputation, and took upon him the form of a servant, and was made in the likeness of men: And being found in fashion as a man, he humbled himself, and became obedient unto death, even the death of the cross. Wherefore God also hath highly exalted him, and given him a name which is above every name.

My goal is for us to discover together what it means to think like Christ. And, as always, our primary tool for doing this will be the Word of God. Paul addresses the deity of Jesus before He came to earth. He talks about Jesus being in the form of God because He did exist in word form with God in the very beginning.

A lot of people get confused with this "thought it not robbery" part, so I want to address it for a moment. There's no disadvantage in claiming to be a child of God. Even though they might try until they're blue in the face, nobody can disenfranchise you on account of that. When you claim that you are a child of God, you are not robbed of anything at all. You are saying, "I am a child of God who was bought by the blood of Jesus." That's an advantage if I've ever heard one!

A lot of you think obedience is just for Sundays. Obedience isn't something that you are supposed to whip out when you feel like it. It's an all-the-time thing. And this obedience that Jesus displayed is what led to His exaltation.

Countless things are vying for our attention nowadays. That's what TV is all about. People can't get any work done without a pair of headphones in their ears playing background music. There are so many distractions we have to deal with that we need a stronger, louder one in order to shut them out. And the stronger, louder a distraction is, the less likely you are to hear what's truly important.

Something that makes Christianity stand out on a global scale is the transition of Jesus from deity to man. John 1:14 says, "And the Word was made flesh, and dwelt among us, (and we beheld his glory, the glory as of the only begotten of the father,) full of grace and truth." Jesus existed in word form first, but then, He became a physical presence on the planet.

He had a brain and a heartbeat just like you do. He had hands and feet just like you do. But in order to make

Himself of no reputation, Jesus had to become what He wasn't. He could have come down to earth with all kinds of accolades and status, but He didn't. He was born into a poor family and eventually became a carpenter. That's a serious step down, if you ask me.

Anyone who truly adopts a Jesus mindset is never solely worried about their own agenda. They are willing to stay in the background. Not a lot of people like to fade into the background because we all want credit for what we're doing. But even if you are in the front, on the side, or wherever else God puts you, it's not about you.

Jesus was born to the poorest man in town. He was born in a city that had never produced anyone famous. He took one of the lowest-class jobs available. Jesus initially created the trees that wood comes from, and then when he was born as a human, He began building chairs with it. He was even able to humble Himself under Joseph, His earthly father, whom He created in the first place!

If you want to witness some power, remove yourself from your pedestal and let God take the top spot. Then you will see real power in action. Jesus was able to humble Himself so radically because He understood that the transformation would please God. Some of us haven't reached that realization yet, and that's why we struggle.

You cannot serve God based on what it's going to get you. You serve Him based on what it's going to do for Him. A lot of people say they're doing things for the glory of God, but they're not sincere. You know you don't like serving, but you just say you're doing it for God's glory because it makes you feel good. Humility is not a position—it all has to do with our mindset. I can physically bow down in front of God all I want, but in my mind, I am standing up. Am I kneeling in my thinking?

Now, the only way any person can come into the world is through the womb of a woman. And as you know, every woman who had a baby had a husband. Here's the tricky part: God couldn't let Mary birth Jesus by a man, not even Joseph, her intended husband.

So, God basically said, "I found the right girl, and now I'm going to clone myself. I'm going to place Myself as a seed in her womb. I'll have the Holy Spirit fertilize Me, and then I'll birth Myself into the world. I don't want any man to do it, and I don't want to involve any woman who isn't a virgin. I have to do this part Myself."

But when Jesus came out of Mary's womb, His umbilical cord had to be cut. And they didn't have any plastic bottles back then, which means that she had to breastfeed Him. She was not allowed to have sex with her husband or get pregnant any other time, because that would contaminate her body. She had to be completely sterile, not only during conception, but reproduction and feeding as well. She was not allowed to be contaminated until Jesus was weaned and didn't need anything else from her physically.

It can be hard to imagine Jesus being born in the fashion of men. He made himself of no reputation. You and I could never do that. We say things like, "When I get to heaven, I'm going to be a king over there." Really? If you're going to be king, what is Jesus going to be?

Heaven is not about you. It's not about being reunited with your loved ones, either. All they do in heaven is worship. And in case you didn't know this already, you and I will not be the main topic of worship. "When I get to heaven, I'm going to put on a new robe." No, you are not! They probably don't wear robes in heaven. If they do, the only person who wears one is Jesus.

When He walks into the room, the ceiling looks like crystal glass, and angels are flying around singing, "Holy, holy." But when Jesus comes to earth, He has to dethrone Himself. What a reversal.

If He existed with God, that means He existed in spirit form. But now that He's on earth, He finds himself like me. As He realized that His outward appearance had changed, He had to undergo a mindset shift. He humbled Himself and became obedient. You can always spot a humble believer because they are in agreement with the Word of God.

He became obedient until when? Death. For lack of a better phrase, you could say Jesus died twice. He had to die from deity, to become flesh, and then had to die in the flesh to give us life.

Christ finds Himself looking just like His creation. His mindset allows Him to be obedient to the word of God, which is what He was in the beginning. Notice that you don't see anything in the text about God making Him obedient. No, He humbled Himself and became obedient. If you want a mindset like Christ's, that's a decision you are going to have to make on your own.

But we pray all the time, "Father, change my mind."

God says "No, I'm not doing that. You can change your mind, and then I'll come beside you and will exalt you as a result of that decision."

No matter what the word of God says, Jesus was always in compliance with it. You have to look at the path He was about to tread in order to get a little context. He became obedient unto death, even the death of the cross. Why? Because when a mind is humbled before God, it is open to whatever God desires.

That's why, in the garden of Gethsemane, Jesus kept saying, "If it be possible." In other words, is there an alternate plan? He wasn't trying to get out of it. He said, "not as I want, but as you want." Basically, he was saying, "If it's not going to happen, I'm good. If it is going to happen, I'm good, because I gave up my mindset a long time ago."

The church today still has serious issues with the vision Jesus has for it and what it wants for itself. Not many want to conform to the image of God. They will conform to anything else they read or hear or see, but they do not want to conform to the God of the universe. It's probably because they know that if they do, it's no longer about what they want to do, it's about what He wants to do through them.

When a person encounters God for the first time in their life, there should be humility there. When Paul met Him, there was humility. When Moses met Him, there was humility. When David met Him as a young boy, there was humility. When Mary met Him, there was humility. What's wrong with us? Today, we show up at church and do the formal thing. Many of us say the prayer and then go back out into the world and make the same mistakes we always make.

Our culture is constantly reinforcing the act of thinking of ourselves first, which makes everyone and everything else just an afterthought. We keep trying to serve God with our mindset the way it is instead of growing into a new one that will humble us and equip us to serve Him.

When our bills come in the mail, we transition into a "lack" mindset. We think, "I gotta do what I gotta do to make ends meet." But that's not a God mindset. You were never supposed to just make ends meet. We have to learn how to depend on God to supply for us in accordance with His riches and glory.

God doesn't make ends meet, because that implies that you only have just enough to scrape by. You don't serve a God who has barely enough; you serve a God who has more than enough. I don't want my ends to meet anymore. I want to have enough rope to get all my needs met and still have enough left over to meet yours too.

The night before Jesus was crucified, in Matthew 26:39, you see a man experiencing real anguish. Even though you love God, some things are going to cause you anguish. If that's true even for Jesus, you better know it applies to us just the same.

A lot of people will have you believe that nothing will bother you because you love Jesus. But even though Jesus already knows what is going to happen, He is still in anguish. It doesn't mean He's going to change His mind or back out of the deal, though. Anguish is simply what human beings feel when they are going through hell.

When a believer is experiencing anguish, he or she will do what a believer is supposed to do: Talk with God about it. Even though Jesus had the faith and the ability to stop it all, He still discussed it with God. If we were in His shoes, and we had the power He did, we'd put a stop to the whole crucifixion deal altogether.

The believer has to understand why certain things are happening in their life. He already knew He was going to Calvary. But the anguish had to do with the cruelty He was about to experience. Jesus fell on His face and prayed, "If it's possible, can we alter the plan? I'm not changing my mind, but is there any room for switching things up and going with Plan B?" Remember, He is not divine. He is human. If He were divine, He would have had an alternate route. But He was human at this point, so He had to talk with God the same way you and I do.

But when He says He wants the cup taken from Him, He doesn't forget to follow up with, "Nevertheless, not as I will, but as You will." The believer always places himself under the authority of the Word of God. Whatever the Word of God dictates, I'm cool with that. Whatever the Word of God requires of me, I'm cool with that, even if it means that I'm going to have to go through some persecution.

Most of the church's problems are not a direct reflection of following the will of God. Instead, they're a direct reflection of us following our own will. And a lot of the time, we're doing that to avoid responsibility or persecution. When we look back on our lives, all the trouble we ran into was a result of refusing to change our mindset and yield to the Word of God. We always find a comfortable way to explain away the mess we made too. "God knows my heart." Yes, He does, and He knows it's not right.

Liberation from the bondage of sin and death requires a different mindset. When you are finally freed from captivity, you need a new mindset to navigate that freedom.

That's what the story of the prodigal son is all about. He left, and even though he was free to do whatever he wanted to do, he did not have the mindset to navigate that newfound freedom. Therefore, he got into all kinds of riotous living. He was irresponsible with his money, with his choices, and with his friends. Even though he thought he was having a good time smoking weed, drinking, and having sex, he wound up with nothing at the end of the day.

So here's Jesus, praying, "Not as I will." Here's a Man who is highly developed in His faith. The Bible tells us that Jesus had the authority to call a legion of angels, so there's no question that He could have stopped the whole process. But Jesus chose to submit to the will of God instead of relying on His own power.

The text doesn't say we have to agree with God's plans, but we sure have to obey them. And what's funny is that, if you're obedient to them, you will wind up liking them.

We don't like to accept our duties when they involve any form of persecution. We think, "As long as nobody questions what God is doing, and as long as I don't experience any challenges, my mindset is with God. But the minute I start having a few difficulties, and things don't go right or the way I think they should, I'm going to alter

God's plan a little bit. The day we got married, everything was fine! When we were on our honeymoon, everything was fine! And then, all of a sudden, everything went south. God, I'm just going to make some minor adjustments to your plan so that it flows a little more smoothly."

Look at what Hebrews 5:8 says about Jesus. "Though he were a Son, yet learned he obedience by the things which he suffered." Do you see that capital S? That implies that Jesus is God's Son. And in the face of that, He still suffered and had to adapt and learn, just like we do every single day.

If Christ had to learn obedience through suffering, so will we. Jesus is the prototype, right? It's not that we have to like it—it's just the process that God has established. This idea of thinking that we're immune to suffering is not founded in the Word at all.

Our God is not a God of suffering. He can't be a God of suffering and a God of healing at the same time. That's contradictory. He can't be a God of misfortune when He is a God of health and prosperity. Instead, He uses Satan's arsenal, with regulations. Yes, God lets him touch you, but only as it suits His plan for you and me. He lets Satan touch you just enough to teach you something and inspire growth, but nothing beyond that.

Look at the limits God puts on Satan in the case of Job. "You can touch him, you can lay your hands on whatever you want, but don't touch his life." God has everything to do with every persecution you face, but those trials are designed to help you grow, not kill you. God is faithful, and

115

He will not allow you to be tested beyond your limitations. And He knows those limitations better than we ever could.

Our God is a God of grace. He uses suffering to grow us into what He wants us to be. I have to look at suffering as an opportunity, even though we all tend to look at it as a disadvantage. If you don't want to be sick, then speak words of healing over yourself. By faith, you are healed. Affliction only lasts until you learn how to stop it. And God always has a reward in store for those who can make it through to the other side of victory.

Now, I can guarantee you, most people you serve are not going to appreciate your service. But you don't do it for appreciation. You do it out of obedience to God. It's going to take some growing to be able to hug somebody while they are cussing you out. It's going to be hard to be nice to a coworker when you know they hate your guts. They can't stand you, but you have to love them anyway.

At work tomorrow, you should buy them lunch. "I'm not buying anybody lunch if they hate me." But we hated God, remember? And that didn't stop Him from sending Jesus. When we metaphorically needed lunch, He didn't turn His back on us. He gave us just what we needed. It's difficult for us to separate our mindset from the ways of this world, but we need to do so if we want to live like Jesus.

Jesus sacrificed a lot to fall from deity to man. He chose to submit Himself to obedience to the Word of God until God said there's nothing left for Him to do. This mindset automatically puts Jesus at the forefront of everything that God has, so He is exalted and given a name above all names. Jesus' humility and obedience is what directly led to that.

Jesus earned the right to say, "I am the way, the truth, and the life. Nobody comes to God except through me." He set the example of what God requires of everyone who worships Him—namely, they must understand suffering and still stay obedient. They must remain faithful to God through adversity and persecution.

Peter is the perfect person to listen to when it comes to mindset changes. Out of all the disciples, he was the one that had to undergo the most dramatic shift. He was an outspoken and violent man. Even when he met Christ, he wasn't any better. Up until he received the Holy Ghost, Paul had to correct him several times for hypocrisy.

"When the Jews aren't around, you eat pork and everything else. When the Jews come around, all of a sudden, you don't eat goat and steak anymore." Paul says, "I don't like people who pretend like that. You are messing these young believers up. If you want to be one way, be that way, but don't try to be both ways at the same time."

At the end of Peter's life, they wanted to crucify him, and he said, "No, I'm not arrogant anymore. I don't deserve to be crucified like Jesus. If you have to kill me, flip me upside down. I'm not even worthy to die in representation of him, because my mind has changed." When you humble yourself, and your mind is made new under the mighty hand of God, who will exalt you? God. But He will not exalt pride, arrogance, or selfishness. However, he is looking to exalt obedience and humility.

You might be wondering what exaltation looks like. A lot of the time, when we think about God exalting us, we want it to be spiritual in nature. We want to lay hands on the sick and heal them at once. But it's different for everyone. He might fix your marriage or get you back into school. God isn't limited to just one method, and we get so busy searching for the miraculous that we miss the obvious.

We always want the exaltation in any form we can win it, but we don't want to be humble. We need to hunger for that exaltation so that the people around us can see our good works and glorify God Himself. It's not about us, but it is up to us to change our mindset. We need to clean out our closets and clean them well.

7

A WORD-WORKING MINDSET

Romans 12:2

No one makes any change in their life, whether it's positive or negative, without having to undergo a mindset shift. This is true for every single transition that you will ever make in your life.

In a church setting, pretty much the only time we discuss mindset transformations is when they pertain to the order of service and Bible study attendance. And then when it comes time for us to actually behave like the church and become the church, we have a difficult time with it. We don't have any problem with saying the right words and clapping and shouting when we're supposed to. We just copy those things from the people around us whenever we get a little lost, and everything turns out fine.

When Jesus told the disciples, "Follow me and I will make you fishers of men," they didn't have any clue about what was going to happen to them. They dropped what they were doing right then and there to follow Him. Jesus had to turn them into what they were not, so they made all sorts of silly mistakes throughout their transformation. They asked a lot of dumb questions over and over again about the same thing. Even though they were physically with Jesus, they still had some more climbing to do in their minds.

We all know that Moses went to Pharaoh in Egypt to bring the children of Israel out. The Bible says that God showed them all kinds of signs and wonders with a mighty hand. But still, they grumbled and complained and found fault with whatever was in front of them. They were always comparing Egypt with where they were. They even had the audacity to claim that slavery was better than being free with God! We can see now how that behavior was the result of an enslaved mindset.

Prison does something to a person. The longer you're locked up, the more comfortable you get behind those bars. That's exactly what the enemy wants. That's the enemy's deepest desire for us. If he can get us involved in things that will hold us hostage, then he can manipulate our mindset. Because, whether you realize it at the moment or not, your mind will change. It kind of kicks in as a survival instinct.

And yes, even the church has to undergo a mindset change. If we are going to be attractive to the world, we have to be ready to receive them on their terms. These people don't know how to talk like you. They don't have the clothes to dress like you. Some of them may not even have the soap and water to bathe and smell like you. They don't understand spiritual things like you claim to understand them. Unsurprisingly, they come in making mistakes, and it's up to us to receive them and welcome them.

God received us when we didn't have soap or water, didn't He? Why is it that we are never willing to do for others what God did for us? Why is it that we are seldom willing to put ourselves out on a limb for somebody else the way He does for us? That tells us something about our mindset as the church. You say, "They ought to be this way!" You weren't. "They ought to know this!" You didn't. But God was patient with us. He used someone to teach us when we didn't want to learn. It wasn't too long ago that none of us knew anything at all about what God required of us, but now that we have a little knowledge of God's Word, we are reluctant to show patience to others.

How can you adopt a kingdom mindset when you're living with a mindset of selfishness? When you need a hand, you want God and the angels and everybody on the planet to stop what they're doing and help you out. But when it's somebody else's turn, you don't have the time, the patience, or the resources. Really?

Let me tell you what people of the world think about church people. First of all, they think we are phony. I don't know if you know that, but it's true. They look at us like people who try to be something that we are not but will still manage to find fault with someone else for trying to be something they are not.

When people of the world look at the church, they think in terms of the building, not the people. They think that, because we hang around this building, there ought to be something different about us. They don't know how we should be different; they just know that we ought to be different. But then we open our mouths, which changes the whole scenario. A lot of folks don't want to bother with us or migrate over here because they don't see any real difference between us and the world. We can be a rebellious people, you know. Being inside of a church building doesn't make us immune to rebellion.

In this chapter, I'd like to discuss what Paul means when he writes about a petrified mindset. This is especially interesting coming from him because when Paul speaks, you wouldn't think he'd know the first thing about it. It just doesn't seem plausible that a man like him would have a mission like that. But the word "petrified" in this context has to do with an organic substance that has hardened. For example, dinosaur bones are petrified. All the marrow has escaped, and they've become these hard-cased fossils like a rock.

Unfortunately, the mind can become just like that if you are not careful. People get involved in things they have no business touching. No one ever desires to become a drug addict. They don't wake up one morning and say, "I'm going to become a drug addict!" It starts out with having some fun or relieving some stress. But somewhere along the way, something changes. The drug they're using gets ahold of their mindset, and their mind becomes so petrified that addiction can sneak in without being noticed.

We know that being saved gets you an eternal existence all by itself. But our dilemma is much more apparent in our daily life. When I was growing up in church, I was taught that all I was supposed to work for was heaven's reward, but that was never true. I don't have to work for heaven's reward. No, all I had to do was speak myself into that. The work had already been done on the cross. I wish someone would have told me that the majority of the work would need to take place in my everyday life.

In essence, we came to church as a formality. A relationship with Christ was not part of our life. Instead, going to church was part of our life. We went to church and did all the things that made us look like we were okay. But once we left the building, we continued to party just like the other crowd. We were never challenged with having to change our mindset.

Everybody would say, "That's so wrong," but they never said, "This is how you fix it. This is how you change it. This is how you come up out of that." They never helped. They were quick to complain about what we were doing, but they'd never give us information or ammunition to nudge us in the right direction. So here we are in our 50s and 60s, and boy, it is hard to teach an old dog new tricks.

Human beings are creatures of habit. When we pass a certain age, we don't want to be bothered with changing our mind. We worked our whole life and finished our career. We finally have some social security and pension coming in. We drive a decent little car that's paid for, and our mortgage is pretty squared away. Why change now?

I wish I had somebody to help me with change. I don't want to change anything. I have become accustomed to me. I know what I like and what I don't like. I know whom I like and whom I don't like. I know what I want to say, because I say pretty much anything I want to say, and now you have the nerve to show me where the Word says that I need a new mindset? You don't know how long it took me to get like this.

Just because the church meets and spends an hour together doesn't mean that it's thriving. A thriving church is a group of people who are operating successfully in line with the scriptures. They don't just have evidence that they're going to heaven—they have His assurance that they are the children of God.

What happens when we are involved in things that get so ingrained in us that they harden our minds to the point where we can't receive from God? We develop a hardened mindset about things that are not of God, and then we fight against God when He comes to us with things that are of Him.

God is always doing something different with us, but it's difficult for Him to move us from point A to point B because we are creatures of habit. We protest, "I just got here. I like it here. Things are working here. I don't want to leave." But God is telling us that the tour doesn't end here. This is just where we start the next part of our journey. He has bigger and better plans for us, but we want to settle down right here for comfort's sake.

Let's go back to Ephesians 4:17-19. Paul is warning the church against being like the Gentiles. The church was comprised of Gentile believers, and he didn't want them to have the same mindset as the Gentiles who are not believers. Paul says,

This I say therefore, and testify in the Lord, that ye henceforth walk not as other Gentiles walk, in the vanity of their mind, Having the understanding darkened, being alienated from the life of God through the ignorance that is in them, because of the blindness of

their heart: Who being past feeling have given them-
selves over unto lasciviousness, to work all uncleanliness
with greediness.

We know by now that there should be a visible difference in the way the people of the church live out their lives
as opposed to folks who are not of God. The word "vanity"
here means being empty and worthless. A lot of these
Gentiles thought they were model citizens, but they really
had no idea how to live according to God's Word.

A person can think they have it going on with God, but
what are they using as a rubric? If you are measuring that
by comparing yourself to the people around you, you're way
off base. Whether you are operating in your own empty-
mindedness or in the mind of Christ, the Word is the best
measuring stick. Paul isn't trying to get the believers to
compare themselves to the people of the world but rather to
the way that God sees them.

If we try to measure up with the people around us, we
will always find a way to justify our behavior. We'll say,
"Well, I'm not as good as her, but at least I'm not as bad as
him." As long as we keep doing that, Christ isn't the main
focus of our lives. When we line ourselves up against Him,
it is clear that He sets the perfect example of how we are
supposed to be. I think that's what Ephesians is all about.
Christ is the model. It's not about this church or that de-
nomination. Jesus is the way, period.

Many times, the old man mindset has a tendency to
make us believe things about ourselves that are scripturally
untrue. Why? Because we don't want to feel bad. We want

to feel good. So, who better to lie to me than me? Do you know what counselors do? They try to help you stop lying to yourself. Because after a while, you begin to believe your own lies, and the truth becomes blurrier and blurrier.

Turn to Ephesians 2:1-2. Paul says,

And you hath he quickened, who were dead in trespasses and sins; Wherein in time past ye walked according to the course of this world, according to the prince of the power of the air, the spirit that now worketh in the children of disobedience.

The word "quickened" here means that we've been brought to life. We were dead in sin and trespasses, but now we are alive again. Everybody can remember when the devil called the shots. And when he told us to do something, he never had to say it twice, because we were all over it.

Sometimes, when you look at the church, you wonder what spirit is working there. When we look at our own lives and the things we do and the words that come out of our mouths, we wonder the same thing. Are we operating in a spirit of disobedience? We say one thing and do the opposite. "Well, you have to be this way so that the world will see you." No, we were taught to distance ourselves from the world. But the church became so inwardly focused that we started having testimony parties and only inviting ourselves.

We were told not to associate with the "others." That presents a real problem because Jesus associated with all sorts of folks that we don't want anything to do with. At every church Paul planted, he was among them. How are you going to plant churches in darkness and watch the

Savior of the world associate with folks in darkness, but then allow the modern church to completely separate itself from the people in the world?

We can't do that. If we have tasted Him and found Him to be good, then we should want everyone else to taste Him too. Paul tells us that we have been set free and brought to life. This might ruffle some feathers, but a "holier than thou" mindset is in the same cup as a wicked mindset. There's no difference between the two. Thinking that we are so holy and righteous that we don't have to associate with anyone else will petrify our mind to the point where it starts to believe the same lies. Remember that God can use us to affect change wherever He has placed us.

We can't operate in vanity anymore because we've been made alive. This is one of the key ideas to keep in mind about the trespasses and sin that caused our death. Because they're so customary and culturally accepted, we often can't see them in ourselves.

Let's use cigarettes as an example. Awhile after nicotine came onto the scene, manufacturers had to start putting a warning label on the packages. It basically said, "You do know what you're getting into, right?" All these folks were coughing and hacking, but they still kept smoking. They became addicted to the nicotine in the cigarette, which changed them from simply wanting a cigarette to needing one. When I want a cigarette, I grab one whenever I feel like it. But when a cigarette tells me I have to have it, it drives me to get one, whether I want it or not.

Sins and trespasses have a way of addicting us. In addictions, it seems like your body is craving the substance that you are addicted to, but it's really not. It's actually your mind that wants it, and it's telling your body to do whatever it takes to get it. After a while, your mind says, "No, we are not quitting because you are not ready to stop. It's easier to just keep on going."

Paul says that we have been delivered from that darkness, that cycle of addiction. We had to be delivered from it because when your understanding is darkened, there's no way we can deliver ourself, or even realize that we need deliverance in the first place.

My father was an alcoholic. We didn't know about alcoholism back then, but we did know that he drank a lot. Actually, he only did it on Fridays. But then I found out that there's something called a Friday drunk. He'd spend his whole paycheck on one day of drinking.

My father started drinking in his early teens. Back then, people thought that teaching boys to become men meant handing them a shot of moonshine. They thought it'd put some hair on their chest. But after years of doing that, it all came full circle. At the ripe old age of 47, he found himself lying on an apartment floor, stabbed in his heart, bleeding to death. When your mind becomes hardened to the things that are right and open to the things that are wrong, the wrong things want nothing more than to drive you to death.

We hear a lot about darkened understanding and alienation in divorce. Being estranged means feeling separated from somebody you used to love. People who are not saved are estranged from God. You might say, "But they didn't use to love God." Yes, they did. They had a relationship with God long before this one. These nonbelievers are alienated from the love and the life of God.

For the most part, people won't come to Christ because they don't see themselves in bad shape. But they're only measuring themselves against the people around them. If they try to compare to the people in church rather than the Word, they'll probably feel like they're doing just fine. These people outside of the church are alienated from God through ignorance and blindness of heart. They don't know, and they can't see. Their hearts are so severely calloused that they are no longer receptive to the Word or the love of God.

When you first start using a shovel, you have some nice smooth hands, don't you? Unfortunately, you have to go through some pain to develop hands that are calloused enough to handle the shovel for any length of time. From repeated use, you literally break your hands down.

Before a callous forms, blisters appear. On your very first day of using a shovel, you'll have blisters by sundown. Even if you wear gloves, blisters will show up. And when they do, you burst them, but you have to go back to work the very next day. On day two, your hands begin to fortify themselves to keep the blisters from appearing again. To develop a calloused mindset, you put yourself through literal hell. Your body has to do something within itself to respond to what you are doing, so the pain won't be so unbearable that you can't move forward.

Our bodies say, "Look, we need to do something about these blisters that keep forming. When they burst, they are sensitive and sore. It hurts so much! We should just callous our hands to make them so hard that they won't feel the shovel when we're digging." That's what the mind does too. It will find a way to make the pain more bearable. It will petrify itself to what is right because you are steadily feeding it what is wrong.

There aren't a lot of lotions that can fix calloused hands. You know what can actually help more than any product on the market? Time away from whatever made them calloused. The same principle works for your mind. You have to give your mind an opportunity to heal so you can present it with something different.

The order of operations goes like this: First, there's a darkening of understanding. Then, there's an alienation from God because of ignorance, followed by a blindness of the mind. I firmly believe this happens in believers and non-believers today.

Romans 1:21 says, "Because that, when they knew God, they glorified him not as God, neither were thankful; but became vain in their imaginations, and their foolish heart was darkened." Do you know how many of us in the church gladly receive His blessings every day but then don't glorify Him as God? We don't show gratitude for what we are given. Sometimes, we take God for granted in the same way that we take His blessings for granted. And when that happens, we are operating within a mindset that's different from what God requires to serve Him. Our reasoning must be sound and in line with the Word of God.

Most kids these days are not accepting of truth like my generation was. They don't believe whatever their parents say as we did. Instead, they question every little thing we say and somehow find fault with all of it. But then, when someone at school tells them a lie, they don't question it at all. Back in the days of Jesus, society was the same way. They were doubting the truth and accepting all of the wrong things without ever stopping to think about what they were doing.

Remember, Satan doesn't force anybody to participate. He only presents a proposal. That's all he does. He makes a presentation of what he wants you to partake in. You have to volunteer to participate. And when you do, he doesn't tell you what the ramifications are.

Our flesh loves all the wrong things. We have to be reconditioned with a mindset that loves right and hates wrong. Now, we weren't made like that. We have to learn how to love God. We didn't have to learn to love the devil, though. We were born with that. We never had to teach ourselves to do the wrong thing. It was automatic.

That's what Paul says in Romans 7: "I find this struggle going on in me. Every time I want to do good, evil is present." That's our dilemma today. We have a desire to do right all the time, but evil is always hanging around. Even when we push through and do right, it says something like, "You got away that time. But I will be here next time, so don't you worry about that."

See, most believers will say, "I just do the right thing all the time. God is my strength. Yeah, He just blesses me, and I'm able to carry on. I'm not worried about the devil's opposition." You know they're not telling the truth! If that were the case, why does Paul talk about struggling with this? There is a constant war in your mind over what you're going to do next. There's a part of us that loves to do wrong, and it's always looking for ways to interfere with the part of us that loves to do right.

This is exactly why we need to encourage each other. All of us have the same problem in this arena. Every time we're faced with right, wrong shows up uninvited. It's always there to crash our right parties, our right relationships, and our right plans. And instead of pretending we have it together, wouldn't it be so much better to let people know that they're not alone in that fight?

In our society today, we label as sickness everything we participate in that becomes an addiction later on. We call alcoholism a sickness. But remember how you got to that point? You willfully participated when you started drinking. The devil just makes a proposition. That's all God does too. If you accept Christ, that's all you. When He presents an opportunity, and we say yes, we receive Him. It's that simple.

The devil doesn't come and snatch me. I walk right through his door. He doesn't come out here and kidnap me. No, he drops a few crumbs and presents me with an opportunity. If I see them and I want to taste one, I can do that. And so he just keeps dropping crumbs, and when we pick them up we are giving ourselves over to the very things that harden our mindset.

And when we become hardened in our mindset to what

is right and comfortable with what is wrong, we are past feeling in a sense. The sins and trespasses don't seem so bad anymore because we're familiar with them. And when a person has turned themselves over to what is unrighteous, only the power of righteousness can bring them back.

This is what happened on the day that over 20,000 Israelites were consumed by fire. They were so engrossed in an orgy that they completely forgot where they were and even who they were. All of those trespasses were taking place in the presence of God.

As a result, God told Moses in Exodus 32:7, "And the Lord said unto Moses, Go, get thee down; for thy people, which thou broughtest out of the land of Egypt, have corrupted themselves." When we hand ourselves over to unrighteousness, our thinking becomes corrupted, and that's where addictions come from. That's where murders come from. That's where all these hate crimes come from. The criminals have become so petrified that wrongdoing doesn't even register with them anymore.

Any psychologist will tell you that the mind will fortify itself in whatever way it can to stop the pain of what is being done to the person. That's why you have split personalities. The mind will develop whatever it needs to develop to deal with the pain.

Today, the spirit of rebellion is so strong among God's people in the church that most congregations can't get anything done. They have 1,000 people at their disposal, but everyone is running in a different direction. They all refuse to be under control or unified in the Holy Spirit.

Have you ever seen another time in our country's history that had this excessive level of sin? When you give yourself over to lust, you do everything in excess. And it becomes so excessive that it's eventually accepted, and the next thing you know, we're voting for it because we can't see the wrong in it anymore.

These people are in the church too, and we have to get them saved just like everyone else! They were around in Paul's day, and they were around in Noah's day. It's not a new problem. And if we're not careful, we might start buying into the lies and become petrified ourselves.

When a culture turns itself over to the excess of unrighteousness, people will commit all uncleanliness and operate in greediness. You know, most cultures in the world want to be like the West. But I'll go over there myself and tell them, "You don't want to be like us." They don't necessarily want to be like we are, but they do want to accomplish what we can accomplish in America. Unfortunately, we are so busy following unrighteousness that we can't actually accomplish anything.

Greedy people want everything they see. And everything they want belongs to somebody else. If you're greedy, you want their woman, you want their man, you want their clothes, you want their house, and you want their congregation. Greed comes from a petrified mind, as well. Paul reminds us to watch out for that.

You might be thinking, "Paul, why are you telling people of God that? This seems like a message you should be preaching outside in the park to the people who are not

Christians." We want to believe that we are immune to becoming hardened in our hearts. But the minute you think you can't have a hard heart, you already have one. What we are doing requires total dependence on God by His Word and His Spirit every day.

For the time past of our life may suffice us to have wrought the will of the Gentiles, when we walked in lasciviousness, lusts, excess of wine, revellings, banquetings, and abominable idolatries (1 Peter 4:3).

Check out 1 Timothy 4:2 as well. "Speaking lies in hypocrisy; having their conscience seared with a hot iron."

In the old west, they didn't have stitches and painkillers. When a person got shot, they would take a branding iron or a knife and put it in the fire. If they could get the bullet out and stop the bleeding, then the person had a good chance of survival. They would let that blade get red hot and press it against the wound. That heat would cauterize the ends of the blood vessels and stop the bleeding.

It's interesting that Timothy would talk about a seared conscience. When we do things we ought not do, a conviction arises in our mindset about it, causing us to be ashamed. When we lose the ability to feel guilty about doing wrong, it's like our conscience has been seared with a hot iron, and we are past feeling guilty. It doesn't bother us anymore. As a matter of fact, it gives us great pleasure. So we continue to live unrighteous as others do, and we feel no conviction.

In Peter's verse above, he's saying that we've done

enough walking in the lifestyle of Gentiles and non-believers. We have paid enough to that old lifestyle, and we never gained a thing from it. All it did was take, take, take; and the more we gave, the more it took.

I believe God is saying, "I sent many representatives, from Genesis to Revelations. And you killed everyone I sent in the Old Testament. Every time a representative told you what I wanted, you gave Me something I didn't want. I even sent Jesus, and you killed Him too. You have always been a rebellious people. You have always had a petrified mindset against righteousness. No matter who I sent, no matter what they said, no matter what proof I provided, you killed every last one of them and returned to savagery. It's time to wake up! Because when I come again, and when Jesus comes again, there will be no more chances. There will only be judgment."

The petrified mind will continue to seek out natural means to fix a supernatural problem until we finally turn back to God.

8

※꒳☆

A PURIFIED MINDSET

Ephesians 4:17-19

In this final chapter, we're going to look at something along the same lines of a petrified mindset but from a different angle. The world is waiting for the manifestation of the sons of God. That's what the scripture says in Romans 8:19, which means that the sons of God have not manifested yet. If that's true, then why do we call ourselves the church? Maybe God is looking for something other than just church folks.

Sons emulate their father. They mimic their father's mindset because he has passed it to them through teaching and leading by example. The world has a right to expect a manifestation of God from those of us who call ourselves His children. And when people look at us and don't see God in us, it's because we are still trying to develop the mindset of our father. That isn't easy, as we've discovered throughout this book.

We do know one thing for sure, though: A changed mindset equals a changed lifestyle. A truly changed mindset will transform our conduct. We have been instructed by scripture to let our light shine before men so they can see our good works and glorify God. This all hinges on an expectation.

You know, I often wonder why God put me where He put me. He and I have discussions about this all the time. There are certain moments when I don't agree with where God put me because things aren't going the way I wish they would. He doesn't pay any attention to that kind of conversation, though. He lets me talk and carry on, but He doesn't change His mind about where He placed me. After a while, I begin to talk to myself, and I eventually remember why I'm here. He says, "I knew you would remember in a minute or two. Now go back in there! I'll see you again in about six months."

Much of the time, we do what we do as a result of how we think. Our approach to life is based on our thought process, which stems out of how we were raised and the people with whom we were associated. If you grew up around people who used profanity constantly, that's all you heard. When you got old enough, you began to participate, and eventually became well-versed in profanity as an adult. As a matter of fact, you could even say profanity is your second language. For many of us, profanity was our first language.

With anything you want to change in your life, progress begins with changing how you think about it. To correct that habit in my speech, my mindset had to be changed. I had to make a conscious effort to turn my speech around, which means I had to alter my view and my thinking about profanity. I no longer saw it as popular and cool. Instead, I saw it as embarrassing. But if you never see it as embarrassing, you will keep on doing it. And the more praise you get for it, the more you will continue and the more proficient you will become in using profanity.

The modern church in America is just like the church in Corinth. In America, we are surrounded and bombarded by evil regularly—TV, internet, newspaper, and so on. At one point, the church in America was what people called the most powerful church in the world. And in many ways, it still is. Technology can get in the way of that, though. We are bombarded with so many distractions that it seems like we are unable to experience any victory against evil.

Meanwhile, overseas, where technology isn't growing as rapidly, people are experiencing God as we have never seen before. They are getting healed, delivered, and set free from demonic strongholds. Folks are even being raised from the dead! I have witnessed this firsthand; strongholds are being broken.

What is the difference between here and over there? Here's a hint: it has to do with their mindset. God has blessed us to the point that we are too comfortable. America is the only country on the planet where you can make all the wrong decisions in life and still end up living somewhere nice and spending money you didn't earn. You can come to America from anywhere and rise to prominence because of the way the democratic process works.

Unfortunately, so many of us don't capitalize on this because we have the wrong mindset. Even though you can be successful in America, the time of America simply giving you everything is slowly and methodically coming to an end. Unfortunately, a lot of folks don't even know it. The American government realizes that we can no longer afford to have almost a third of our citizens on welfare. It's impossible to continually generate that kind of money. We can support those who have birth defects and things of that nature, but those of us who are healthy and able to work need to come up with a new plan.

Other countries already have a plan. In America, so many people want to get on disability. "I didn't do anything, but I want something for free." That's a crooked mindset. Why would anybody want to get on disability in America? You only get about $300 a month. That won't supply enough Wendy's burgers to last you a full month. Even if you get the $300 and all of your medical expenses taken care of, you still can't successfully live on that.

But there's a mindset that goes along with being on disability. "I'm sticking it to the man." People who think that way never realize that they're doing the greatest injustice to themselves. Instead of sitting around, I should pick my lazy self up and get a job or go back to school and graduate. I should do whatever I need to do to change my mindset. Then we have others who champion us for being lazy, saying, "Atta boy! I don't blame you; get that money." Man, you haven't worked a day! I don't believe anybody who hasn't worked should get social security benefits unless they are permanently disabled. If you don't work and pay in, you shouldn't get anything out. God says that if a man doesn't work, he shouldn't eat.

In Ephesians 4:19, Paul says, "Who being past feeling have given themselves over unto lasciviousness, to work all uncleanliness with greediness." We surmise that this is what happened to the Gentiles in Ephesus. Paul was comparing the people inside the church to the people outside of the church. When your mindset becomes petrified or hardened to the things of God, you literally give yourself over to the things of the devil. That's what has happened with many people. That's why we have so much crime. People are killing each other like it's a fad.

A mindset is a powerful mechanism when it's in the wrong hands or the right hands. When a mindset has become pliable to evil, hatred, discomfort, and anger, it does everything to the extreme. Nothing is untouchable; nothing is unreachable; nothing is undoable. But in Ephesians 4:20, he says, "But ye have not so learned in Christ." Wherever you got the idea to behave and think that way, it sure wasn't from Jesus!

That is what trips America up. People look at us and see no real difference between us and those outside of the church. We have a higher divorce rate in the church than in the country as a whole. Eighty percent of families in the church are breaking up. These are folks who love Jesus. Pastors are walking out of pulpits by the hundreds, turning their backs on their assigned calling.

There's no way we can say, "Well, God told me to do this" when it doesn't line up with scripture. You can declare that all you want, but those orders did not come from God or His Word. It has become such a fad because we, the people of God, fall for anything as long as someone puts God's name on it.

Where is the scripture that backs up what you just did? "Well, I didn't know it was going to be like that." Isn't it amazing how the word of God can be read, and everybody takes away something different? Those who are listening with the intent of following hear a different message than those who don't have that intention.

The key to my new conduct is a changed mindset. But when I make that change, it's going to upset the balance of my whole existence. I'll have to learn how to do everything all over again. That taxes me. That puts pressure on me, and nobody wants that, right?

Now, look at verses 21 and 22.

If so be that ye have heard him, and have been taught by him, as the truth is in Jesus: That ye put off concerning the former conversation the old man, which is corrupt according to the deceitful lusts.

Most of us believers are still unable to understand what God is saying in His Word, no matter how many times we read it. We come up with all kinds of strange revelations instead of the intended one because we look at it through the lens of a mind that hasn't been changed. You can't read the Bible like you read any other book.

When people in my area find out my name is Ellis Hodge, you know how they identify me? "Oh, you are Sister Pat's boy." The new age people have a problem with that—they want to be identified as themselves. Really, though, you ought to be glad someone identifies you with your parents because they are the ones who have hopefully given you a godly foundation. Everybody I run into knew my mother. I am proud to be identified with my mother because she had respect in our neighborhood. Along with being associated with my mother and grandmother, I was expected to behave like them.

A lot of us are fighting against the mindset that our parents were trying to give us when we ought to be eating it up. We want to be identified as ourselves, but we haven't been around long enough to establish roots in anything yet. We need to identify with where we came from. "You are somebody's boy. I know your mama. She's a hardworking, honest, God-fearing woman who loves Jesus. Your parents raised you right." Who wouldn't want to identify with that? Whenever I see you, I am expected to demonstrate her.

In my neighborhood, folks see me leaving my driveway with my suit on to go to church every Sunday and shout hallelujah. They think, *He must be going to church. He leaves every Sunday morning. And every Wednesday night, he goes to Bible study.* This makes people see me as different from the rest of the neighborhood.

But if I'm in the front yard cussing at my wife every time I come home from church, I'm confusing everyone who sees me. They expect me to be different. You wouldn't expect a man who spends a few days a week at church to cuss out his wife in broad daylight, would you? People would say, "I don't know what the deal is with this church thing or this Christian thing or whatever y'all want to call it. Everyone he runs with acts the same way."

The world expects us to be like our Father, and they have the right to do so because that's what God expects of us too. If you love Jesus, you ought to show some evidence of it. And no, just going to church isn't really a sign.

To truly love Jesus is to demonstrate Him. In 1 John, Jesus said, "If you love me, you will keep my commandments" and not "If you love me, you will go to church." Then He says, "My commandments are not grievous." Why do we make them hard when they really aren't?

The apostle Paul's encounter with Christ on the road to Damascus was a significant event in his life. Paul had been taught by some of the most astute teachers on the planet, but they only taught him in the law. They didn't teach him about Christ. If they did, he wouldn't have had the encounter in Damascus. They taught him law, so he developed a mindset for the law. That's why he said he had a zeal for it. His mindset was, "I'm going to kill and persecute everyone that's disobeying the law." He targeted believers. The only way his mindset could change from law to grace was through meeting Jesus.

God arranged for Jesus to meet him on the road to Damascus. It's not like Paul just randomly bumped into Jesus. No, Jesus went looking for him. Why? It was time for him to undergo a mind transformation. God knocked him off his beast with a blinding light, and when he woke up, he couldn't see a thing. All God wanted to do was get a message to Paul that he needed to hear. And this encounter wrecked Paul's entire theology. He was blind for three days, but once he regained his sight, his mindset had been overhauled. He immediately set out on a different path.

The world is confused when we say we love God, but our lifestyle doesn't change. For example, maybe you preach to people every Sunday, but you shoot dice all week. Paul changed his whole agenda in life when he regained his sight, but we have trouble doing the same.

Most of us let other folks determine how we are going to live. When Paul was changed, nobody believed it. To this day, he is still referred to as that guy who killed Christians. Don't think the whole world is going to bow down because you switched gears and decided to follow God. They don't know anything about that. They remember what you used to do and how you used to be. That's fine. They need a past to compare with your future.

Paul goes from persecuting Christians to preaching the gospel, from tormenting people to teaching them how to live for God. As a result of that one meeting, God was able to use him to plant churches and write more books of the Bible than anybody else. Some of us have been with Jesus for 40+ years, and we haven't adhered a single word.

Paul maintains that, when an unbeliever looks at us, they assume that we have heard from God. At some point, you get sick and tired of being sick and tired, and you know that you must make some changes. Basically, we didn't learn the way we've been behaving from Christ. And if we really heard and understood His words, then we should already be on the road to change.

When Paul says we should put off the old man, do you know what he means by that phrase? To put something off is to completely quit it. Lay it down. Renounce it. Release it. Cast it off. Quit it once and for all.

Do you have an old garment that you like to put on? There are holes in it because you wear it six or seven days a week, but it's just so comfortable that you can't throw it out. As a matter of fact, when you have washed that garment, you feel incomplete until you put it back on. I used to have a pair of gold jeans that I wore every day. Everybody would always say, "You wear those gold jeans all the time."

I wore them so much that people got tired of looking at me. They couldn't understand why I wouldn't stop wearing those jeans. They fit so well. Eventually, they just wore out. The thread began to rot, and I had to throw them away.

The text is instructing us to lay down the old lifestyle. "But, Pastor, you don't understand." Yeah, I do, because I had to lay it down too. You don't just do it one time, and then you're finished. If it were that easy, we would all be in good shape. Instead, it's a continual process. It's like math. I didn't start learning math in tenth grade but in kindergarten. I had to enter in on the low end of math and work my way through it over time. And as I learned, I built on each concept until I was ready for the next grade. Each year presented a totally new level of math.

Most believers never grow because they are not building on concepts from the scriptures. They keep the same mindset they came in with and maintain that same thought process instead of allowing the learning process to help them grow in the knowledge of the Word of God. It never stops, either. God is always nine million years ahead of us.

We have to be willing to put off concerning our former lifestyle. We have to open ourselves up to be taught differently. A disciple is in love with learning, and he or she understands that they need a teacher to instruct them. That's why Christ told the first disciples, "Follow me and I will make you fishers of men. What you have been doing has nothing to do with what you are going to do." Many of us try to bring our worldly concepts to the table for God to use, unlike His first disciples who had to leave their nets behind. The kind of fishing they were going to do wouldn't require physical nets.

The average church member does not qualify to be a disciple. A disciple isn't just a learner. He is a mimic of his teacher.

If you ask me to mentor your son, that means I'm going to be telling him what he should do, and he should accept the teachable moments. If you don't want that, you don't want a mentor. Jesus says, "Follow me and I will mentor you so that you can become fishers of men. You don't know how to do it, but I do, and I will teach you."

We come to God acting like we know how to do everything. Just because He saved me doesn't mean I'm qualified to do everything, though. Getting saved means that you qualify to go to heaven, but you still don't know how to do anything.

Entering college in your freshman year doesn't qualify you to graduate. You have three more years to prove yourself. Don't start your freshman year trying to act like you're already getting your bachelor's degree. You better use that tutor to get you to the next level. Most of us walk into new territory like we know everything.

But Paul says we have to lay down the old mindset. That's probably going to rub you the wrong way because it certainly rubs me the wrong way. The way I am is the way I am, and now you're trying to tell me I have to lay down 40+

years of doing and experiencing things this way? Yeah, right. But guess what? God expects us to stumble in the changeover.

When we went to basic training in the military, what did we know how to do? Nothing, at first. But by the time they got through training us and running us every time we made a mistake, around week three, we began to understand the process. They had to mold our mindset from civilian to military. Once you get to a certain age, you do what you want to do. When I went to basic training, the first thing I encountered was a small guy shouting at me and daring me to say anything back. He was all up in my face, just yelling. After about three weeks of submitting to the process, I began to move from a civilian mindset to a military mindset. Slowly, I learned how to navigate between the two mindsets.

Most believers can't transition into a different mindset because they have too much rebellion against change. But without a mindset change, there's no change in conduct. And without a change in behavior, you will not live like what you are: a child of God.

Anything that has to do with living in a way that the Bible calls "dark" needs to be cast away. We've all had a taste of dark living. If we never had a taste, Jesus wouldn't have had to come. "What is God after? Does He really expect me to meet Him one day and quit the next?" Yeah. "But that's impossible!" Not really. It's hard, but it's not impossible. It all depends on what you want to do, and in what direction you want to grow.

If I change my thinking immediately, then it makes my heart pliable to receive the seed of the Word of God, which is what causes changes in my life to be possible. But when I'm rebelling in my thought process, it keeps my heart hard, and I'm unable to receive the seed of God's Word that will drive change in my life.

The journey we are about to embark on will not be successful with our old mindset. Every time you want to adopt a new mindset, you need to lay down the old one. If you don't want to pick up the new one, then the old one is what you'll be stuck with.

We've become masters at talking like we want to change. "I'm going to the gym on Monday." But then we wake up late, so we move it to Wednesday. But then something else comes up. Staying dedicated to the gym takes a strong mindset. If you stop going regularly, you get lazy. The whole idea of going back to the gym reminds you that you'll be sore the day afterwards, so you decide not to go at all. But if you finally desire something deeply enough to make a change, you can lay down that old mindset once and for all.

Why don't we need our old nature anymore? Paul says that it's corrupt according to deceitful lust. Our own nature is a corrupt entity. We all used to have very corrupt minds. They were spoiled and defective, so we already know they won't work in our new environment.

When Paul talks about deceitful lust, he means that the old nature is not honest about itself. It tricks us into believing that our current way of living is the right way. And as a result, it tricks us into doing all sorts of things that relate to that unrighteous lifestyle.

When you develop a new mindset, you start doing things differently. Because of that, things around you start happening differently. All your situations are waiting on you to finally change your mindset.

Let's look at Colossians 3:5-9. Paul writes to the church,

> *Mortify therefore your members which are upon the earth; fornication, uncleanness, inordinate affection, evil concupiscence, and covetousness, which is idolatry: For which things' sake the wrath of God cometh on the children of disobedience: In the which ye also walked some time, when ye lived in them. But now ye also put off all these; anger, wrath, malice, blasphemy, filthy communication out of your mouth. Lie not one to another, seeing that ye have put off the old man with his deeds.*

We can see the wrath of God coming down on folks who live that kind of lifestyle. We can't let ourselves participate in it. Paul doesn't let us forget that we used to walk like that, though. But since we aren't like that anymore, we are growing in the right direction. Our relationship with God has changed us.

Seeing that we have put off the old man with his deeds, the next step is to put on the new man, which is renewed in knowledge after the image of God, who created us. We have to develop a new mindset when it comes to fornication, lying, blasphemy, and so on. So many of us aren't able to put off the behaviors associated with our old man, and then we wonder why we aren't operating in the new one.

Many believers pretend to renounce these things but actually don't. "I never lie! I just tell little untruths here and there." We have learned to justify our old nature because we want to keep it.

How many times have you really gotten angry and said something like, "I need to tell you off! I hope God forgives me for it." You know what that is? It's an opportunity to turn the corner. Resisting the urge to shout gives me the strength I need to head in a different direction.

Don't you think you would need a new mindset to give up divinity for poverty? Don't you think you would need a new mindset to allow the folks you created to nail you to a tree? How can we expect to follow Jesus if we don't undergo a mind transformation?

The average person wouldn't want to be poked with a needle, but those of us who have to shoot insulin understand what we are doing and why we do it. We altered our mindset so that we can take a poke from needles every so often and live through it successfully.

You need a new mindset to avoid doing evil for evil. We were born with a nature that dictates, "If you mess with me, I'm going to mess with you twice as hard." God says, "I need a reversal. I need you to renounce that. I need you to lay that down. Change your mindset so we can begin a new process." Christ gives us that great demonstration. You have to leave something behind in order to gain something new.

We need to expect to be involved in the process. We can't expect God to do all of the work. "God, fix me. God, deliver me. God, take me. God, send me." What, are you just going to wait around until He does it for you? God told Moses in Exodus 3:9-10, "I have heard Israel's cry, so I'm sending you back to bring them out. Your message to Pharaoh is that I said to let my people go."

And Moses was living a good life too. Good job, great family, worked for the richest man in the whole kingdom. But when he received the message from God, his mindset changed. For the call of God, he returned to a land he ran away from. I don't know where God is going to send you, but I guarantee you, wherever He sends you, and whatever He does with you, is going to require some serious changes. You simply cannot participate in the things of God with your old mindset.

Even though the whole world may be going to hell in a handbasket, I'm not responsible for the entire world. I'm responsible for me. I have to work hard to keep my head on straight. I have to work hard to keep my mind right. Each day presents new challenges for my mindset, but the Word of God equips me to face them head-on.

About the Author

ELLIS R. HODGE was born in the city of Valdosta, Georgia, to Authur Lee and Elizabeth Hodge. Ellis is a proud graduate of the last all-black high school class of Pinevale High School in Valdosta, Georgia. He attended Valdosta State College until his enlistment in the U.S. Air Force from 1971-1975. Honorably discharged in 1975, he reenlisted in the U. S. Air Force Reserves in 1978, serving with honor and distinction until retiring with honors in 1994.

Ellis worked for GTE/Verizon for 27 years, retiring in 2002. His educational accomplishments include an AA degree from the Community College of the AIR Force in Logistics Mgt., Bachelor of Theology from Christian Faith College, Master of Theology from Life Christian University, Doctor of Divinity from Life Christian University, and Doctor of Divinity from St. Thomas Christian College.

Dr. Hodge is the founder and senior pastor of Word of Life Fellowship Chuch, located in St. Petersburg, Florida, where he has pastored for 22 years. He has been married for 42 years to his supportive and loyal wife, Teralyn Hodge, and they have a son of whom they are very proud, Andrew E. L. Hodge, a precious granddaughter Paxton Andrea Hodge, and a very special and devoted neice, T'nora Renee Dessaw.

Dr. Hodge stands on and believes in completely Romans 10:17, "So then faith cometh by hearing, and hearing by the word of God."

CPSIA information can be obtained
at www.ICGtesting.com
Printed in the USA
BVHW041135160223
658645BV00013B/893